BACK ROADS
OF OREGON

Log barn at Cornucopia

Back Roads of Oregon
by Earl Thollander

Clarkson N. Potter, Inc./Publishers   NEW YORK
DISTRIBUTED BY CROWN PUBLISHERS, INC.

Books by Earl Thollander
BACK ROADS OF NEW ENGLAND
BACK ROADS OF OREGON
BACK ROADS OF ARIZONA
BACK ROADS OF CALIFORNIA
BARNS OF CALIFORNIA

FRONT COVER: Ranch near Galena
on the middle fork of the John Day

Inquiries should be addressed to Clarkson N. Potter, Inc., One Park Avenue,
New York, N.Y. 10016
Printed in the United States of America
Published simultaneously in Canada by
General Publishing Company Limited

Library of Congress Cataloging in Publication Data
Thollander, Earl.
  Back roads of Oregon.
    1. Oregon—Description and travel—1951–
—Guide-books.   2. Automobiles—Road guides—Oregon.
I. Title.
F874.3.T48   1979   917.95'04'4   78-24097
ISBN 0-517-53069-4

I dedicate this book,
with much love, to my
family -- Janet, Kristie,
Wes and Lauren

Contents

Back Roads of Northwestern Oregon

Back Roads of Eastern Oregon

Map legend

• ____3.2____ •   distance in miles between dots

→ → →   my route (which may be reversed should you desire)

▲ campgrounds

■ towns and cities

················· rivers and lake boundaries

□ special location

X my sketching place

⌂ covered bridge

⊤ picnic grounds

✝ cemetery

NORTH is always toward the top of the page

FOREWORD

Oregon is a state with many faces. It is a state of matchless beauty and bountiful resources.

Oregonians are proud of their state. A commonsense approach to problem solving, balanced budgets, and unique environmental laws are all part of the Oregon experience.

Oregon is unique. Mountains, trees, and rocky coves to the west, with deserts and sage to the east. Much of this state's beauty and charm can only be found by the interested explorer who probes beyond the obvious.

Earl Thollander has made a substantial investment of his time and artistic talent in this state. His illustrations and text will convince even the casual reader that there is a valuable reward waiting for those willing to venture off the well-traveled path to search quietly and patiently through Oregon's many special places.

Read and enjoy this guide to the back roads of this state. As governor of Oregon I invite you to experience for yourself the joys of discovery felt by the author as he traveled our country roads. If you have never been to Oregon, I know you will fall in love with our state. If you are a native, a whole new state awaits discovery along the back roads of Oregon.

February, 1979   Governor Vic Atiyeh

Preface

Back Roads of Oregon is a travel guide, an on-the-spot pictorial record of landscapes and places seen, and an effort to give "voice" to the back road beauty of Oregon. For me there is more of nature, more experience of the earth, a greater feeling of history, and more good adventures to be had by getting off the main thoroughfares and away from urban centers.

I drew this book not only because of an urge to describe to everyone what wonderful things I have seen in Oregon, but also to help others, in my small way, discover the beauty of the natural world. Without strong support from concerned people, preserving and managing the natural areas that remain will be difficult. Indeed without care and help we will someday create a less interesting and less habitable planet.

Author's Note

The three parts of *Back Roads of Oregon* begin with a sectional map. This will help to locate the back roads areas on a larger Oregon state map that is available at no charge from many sources, including Travel Services, Chambers of Commerce, Tourist Bureaus and Automobile Clubs. My more localized maps in each section outline every back road and should successfully guide you in your trip. I have put as much information as I could manage into the maps themselves. Arrows show you the direction in which I traveled, although my route could certainly be reversed. The North Pole, unless otherwise indicated, is toward the top of the page. Maps are not to scale because of the diversity in length of the roads; however, mileage notations should help a great deal. My odometer wouldn't have measured distance exactly the same as yours, but their estimates should be similar. Essential to me in following the back roads were sectional maps, which I purchased from the Oregon Department of Transportation, Room 17, Transportation Building, Salem, Oregon 97310. Pasted together, the various sections of a county map, at one-half inch to the mile, would achieve monumental proportions. Malheur County alone, for example, measured 30 x 75 inches! I also purchased maps at ranger stations when entering forest preserves. They are a bit more complete than the Department's sectional maps in that forest road numbers are included.

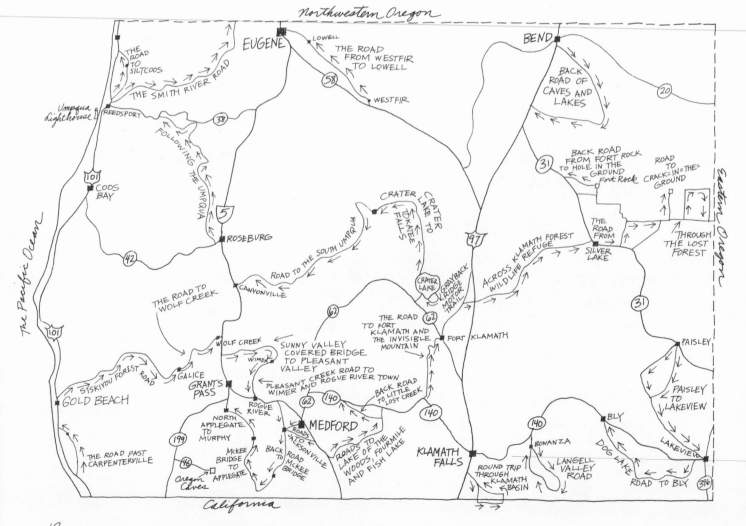

Northwestern Oregon

THE ROAD TO SILTCOOS

LOWELL

THE ROAD FROM WESTFIR TO LOWELL

EUGENE

THE SMITH RIVER ROAD

58

WESTFIR

BEND

BACK ROAD OF CAVES AND LAKES

20

Umpqua Lighthouse

REEDSPORT

38

FOLLOWING THE UMPQUA

31

BACK ROAD FROM FORT ROCK TO HOLE IN THE GROUND

Fort Rock

ROAD TO CRACK-IN-THE-GROUND

101

COOS BAY

THE ROAD FROM

SILVER LAKE

THROUGH THE LOST FOREST

Eastern Oregon

5

ROSEBURG

CRATER LAKE

TOKATEE FALLS

CRATER LAKE TO

97

ACROSS KLAMATH FOREST WILDLIFE REFUGE

31

The Pacific Ocean

42

ROAD TO THE SOUTH UMPQUA

CANYONVILLE

CRATER LAKE

GRAYBACK BRIDGE MOTOR TRAIL

62

THE ROAD TO WOLF CREEK

62

THE ROAD TO FORT KLAMATH AND THE INVISIBLE MOUNTAIN

FORT KLAMATH

PAISLEY

101

WOLF CREEK

SUNNY VALLEY COVERED BRIDGE TO PLEASANT VALLEY

WIMER

PLEASANT CREEK ROAD TO WIMER AND ROGUE RIVER TOWN

BACK ROAD TO LITTLE LOST CREEK

PAISLEY TO LAKEVIEW

SISKIYOU FOREST ROAD

GALICE

GRANT'S PASS

62

140

140

BLY

GOLD BEACH

199

NORTH APPLEGATE TO MURPHY

ROGUE RIVER

ROADS TO JACKSONVILLE

MEDFORD

ROADS TO LAKE OF THE WOODS, FOURMILE AND FISH LAKE

140

140

BONANZA

DOG LAKE

LAKEVIEW

THE ROAD PAST CARPENTERVILLE

146

Oregon Caves

McKEE BRIDGE TO APPLEGATE

BACK ROAD TO McKEE BRIDGE

KLAMATH FALLS

ROUND TRIP THROUGH KLAMATH BASIN

LANGELL VALLEY ROAD

ROAD TO BLY

396

California

12

Rhododendron

Southwestern Oregon

I remember the beauty and force of the ocean coast, the forests gleaming with dew in the morning light, the sumptuous displays of mountain wildflowers, and the textural infinity of sagebrush mixed with pines and junipers in the high, dry portion of southwestern Oregon.

OREGON
CHEDDAR
CHEESE
W. J. WALKER & SON

*cheese factory
at Pistol
River*

The road past Carpenterville

Old Highway 101, called the Carpenterville Road, wound above the ocean through lush, green coastal forest. It becomes a ridge route at times, with long views on both sides of the road, but don't expect a town at Carpenterville!

Just north of Pistol River I drew a picture of a cheese factory of an earlier day being "consumed" by wild blackberry bushes.

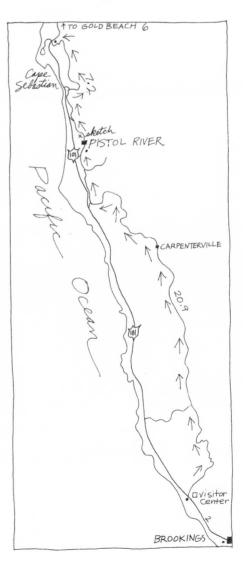

↑ TO GOLD BEACH 6

Cape Sebastian

7.2

× sketch
PISTOL RIVER

101

Pacific Ocean

CARPENTERVILLE

20.9

101

□ Visitor Center

BROOKINGS

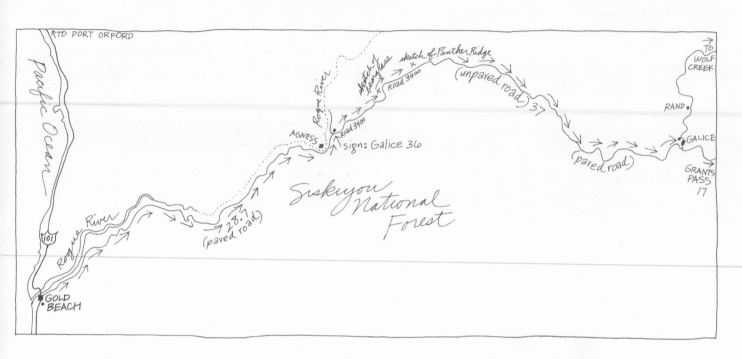

To Port Orford

Pacific Ocean

Rogue River

101

GOLD
BEACH

28.7
(paved road)

AGNESS

Road 3400

sign: Galice 36

Rogue River

sketch of Bearyfass

Road 3400

sketch of Panther Ridge
×

(unpaved road) 37

RAND

TO
WOLF
CREEK

GALICE

(paved road)

GRANTS
PASS
17

Siskiyou
National
Forest

16

Stonecrop

Siskiyou Forest Road,
Gold Beach to Galice

I stopped at Gold Beach
Ranger Station for a
Siskiyou National Forest
map and to ask for
advice on the current
condition of the road
beyond Agness.
The road along the
Rogue River was
paved for the first
twenty-nine miles.
I saw a power boat
moving upstream at
almost the same speed
as I was traveling.
Past Agness a gravel
road wound its way through
the forest. Eventually I
came across an area of many
beargrass plants in blossom.
There, on the white flower I
selected to draw, I discovered
a perfectly camouflaged white
spider that had captured an
unsuspecting wasp.
I had expansive views of
mountains and forest for my
drawing of Panther Ridge.

Beargrass

Panther Ridge

19

WILLIAM
MILLER
—
TENNESSEE
—
20 D E
20,

Headstone at Wolf Creek cemetery

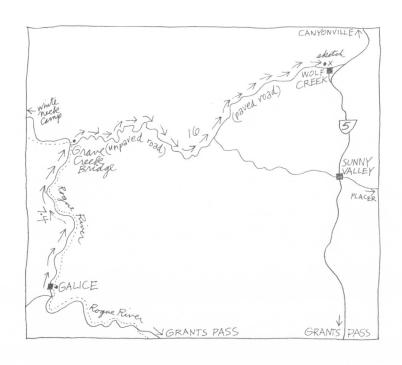

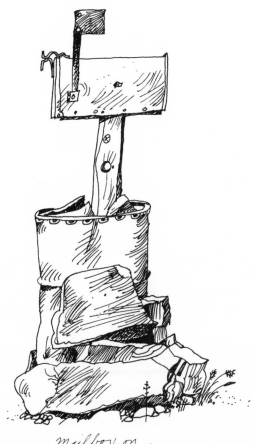

mailbox on
Wolf Creek
road

The road to Wolf Creek

     I took the road north from Galice
along the Rogue, turning east at Grave Creek
Bridge. In five miles I passed a nicely made
log barn and also a sign that said "No shooting
children and livestock." Turning at the fork of
the road toward Wolf Creek, I traveled along
the pretty stream to the sleepy town ahead
where old Wolf Creek Tavern (1857) still stands.
     On a hill nearby I sat in the deep shade
of the town cemetery to sketch an
ivy-covered headstone.

Sunny Valley covered bridge to Pleasant Valley

Sunny Valley covered bridge crosses Grave Creek, so named in memory of a fourteen-year-old pioneer, buried nearby, a member of the first wagon train to enter Oregon by the Applegate Trail in 1846.

A small boy I met who lived on a farm along the road told me that there were beavers in the creek.

I got advice along the way from local folks and abandoned the Daisy Mine Road upon hearing their cautionary "This yere road's so rough ye could berry yer wheel in one 'o them holes."

Meadows along Ditch Creek Road were sprinkled with countless daisies blooming in late spring.

Sunny Valley
covered bridge

23

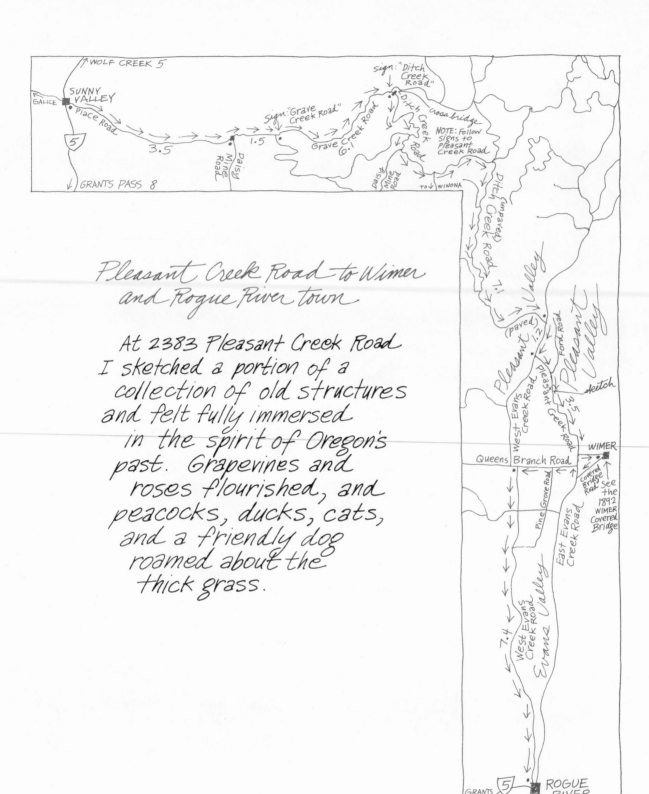

Pleasant Creek Road—to Wimer
and Rogue River town

At 2383 Pleasant Creek Road
I sketched a portion of a
collection of old structures
and felt fully immersed
in the spirit of Oregon's
past. Grapevines and
roses flourished, and
peacocks, ducks, cats,
and a friendly dog
roamed about the
thick grass.

farm on
Pleasant Creek
Road

25

Roads to Jacksonville

Jacksonville is a ghost town revived by a remarkable number of handsome restored houses and other edifices that are worth seeing.

David Rust's place, recognizable by the colossal swans on its porch, is not on the usual tour of Jacksonville.

He said if I brought him the base of a hollow log and the crotch of a tree with the right curve in it, he'd make one for me.

Swan house, Jacksonville

GOLD HILL

5

99

12

62

5.5

5

RUCH 8

238

238

5

238 MEDFORD

99

TO BUNCOM

8

ASHLAND 16

JACKSONVILLE

28 St. Joseph's Church, Jacksonville

Roads to Jacksonville

St. Joseph's Church (1858) at 4th and D streets
in Jacksonville was on the list of things to see.
It's a historical place, as you can tell from
this excerpt from a report by the town's
first Catholic missionary to his superior,
Archbishop Francis Blanchet...

Sept. 18, 1856

... the Catholics in Jacksonville are very
anxious to have a church built amongst
them and are willing to help to the utmost
of their means. I have given them some
hopes of having their wishes realized next
year... Next spring, if the mining be
successful this winter, there would be a fair
chance of making a good collection toward
building a little church, which will
answer not only for that town but for all
the mining districts for 60 or 70 miles
all around.

Back road from Jacksonville to Buncom and McKee Bridge

This was a pleasant trip past stream and forest. At ghostly Buncom cows grazed in the green meadow where the town once stood. Next, I traveled along the Little Applegate River, and then by the big Applegate to McKee Bridge.

The covered bridge was built in 1917 when the Blue Ledge Copper Mine was still transporting ore to Jacksonville.

I could hear the swishing sound of a rotary fish screen operating much like an old-fashioned water wheel as I sketched. The screen prevents trout from going out of the river into irrigation canals and ending up "dried out" in a pasture somewhere.

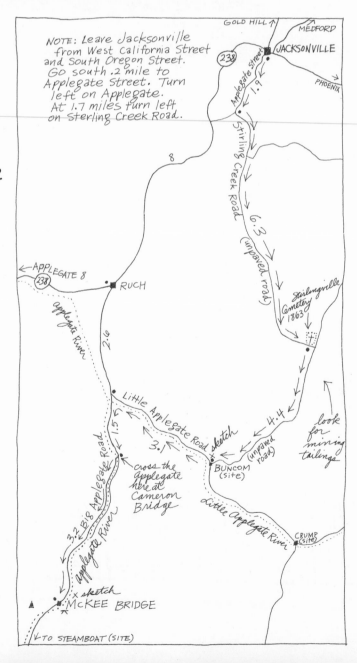

NOTE: Leave Jacksonville from West California Street and South Oregon Street. Go south .2 mile to Applegate Street. Turn left on Applegate. At 1.7 miles turn left on Sterling Creek Road.

GOLD HILL
MEDFORD
238   JACKSONVILLE
Applegate Street
1.9
PHOENIX
Stirling Creek Road
6.3 (unpaved road)
8
Stirlingville Cemetery 1863
←APPLEGATE 8
238
RUCH
Applegate River
2.0
4.4
look for mining tailings
Little Applegate Road   sketch
1.5
3.1
(unpaved road)
BUNCOM (site)
cross the Applegate here at Cameron Bridge
Applegate Road
3.2 B.8
Applegate River
Little Applegate River
CRUMP (site)
× sketch
McKEE BRIDGE
↓TO STEAMBOAT (SITE)

Buncom

33

McKee Bridge to Applegate via Steamboat

Once past the Applegate Lake reservoir the road was picturesque, with meadows, streams and, near the site of Steamboat, with overhanging forest trees. Along Thompson Creek toward Applegate there were many great barns and farms in lovely pastoral settings.

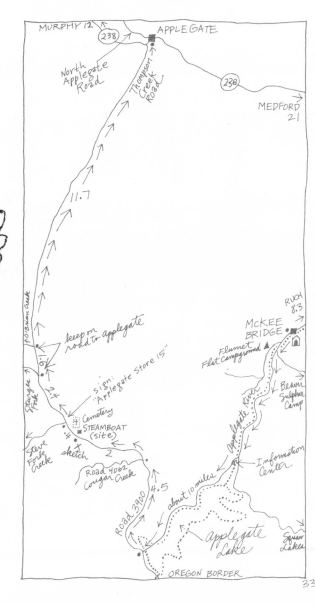

McKee covered bridge

34 The road near Steamboat

The Krause barn, North Applegate Road

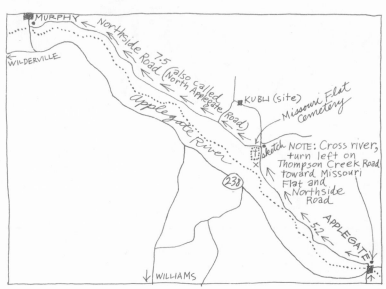

MURPHY

WILDERVILLE

Northside Road

7.5 (also called North Applegate Road)

Applegate River

KUBLI (site)

Missouri Flat Cemetery

sketch NOTE: Cross river, turn left on Thompson Creek Road toward Missouri Flat and Northside Road

238

5.2

APPLEGATE

WILLIAMS

North Applegate Road to Murphy

This byway is also called Northside Road.
It goes past meadows and barns and then idles by
the Missouri Flat cemetery where "Artesian Water
A Gift from God" was offered. In 1943 Bert Clute
donated the water system in memory of his wife, Lydia.
The good water was a gift, indeed.

Roads to Lake of the Woods, Fourmile and Fish Lake

Dead Indian Road, off Highway 66 a mile
or so south of Ashland, is scenic all the way to
Lake of the Woods. Highway 140 off Highway 62
six miles north of Medford goes to Fish Lake,
Lake of the Woods and past the dirt road
turnoff to Fourmile Lake.
There are views of Mt. McLoughlin and I sketched
the classic peak with an early morning mist
mantling its base.
McLoughlin is not a popular name with
old-timers in this area because he favored the
British, so they say. Their name for the
9500-foot mountain was Snowy Butte,
and later, Mt. Pitt.

Mount McLoughlin

Back road to Little Lost Creek

There is a quiet back road paralleling Highway 140 through the Rogue River National Forest. It begins opposite the Big Elk Guard Station near Fish Lake. Ask about the condition of the road at the Guard Station as conditions may vary from season to season and year to year. The road eventually winds (a bit precariously) down into a green valley along the south fork of Little Butte Creek. Southeast of the tiny community of Lakecreek the road past Little Lost Creek branches off one mile to Oregon's "shortest covered bridge."

There was no traffic over the old span as I sketched. A rooster crowed, a fly bit me, green dragonflies whirred by, and spiders lowered themselves onto my drawing paper from an overhanging alder tree.

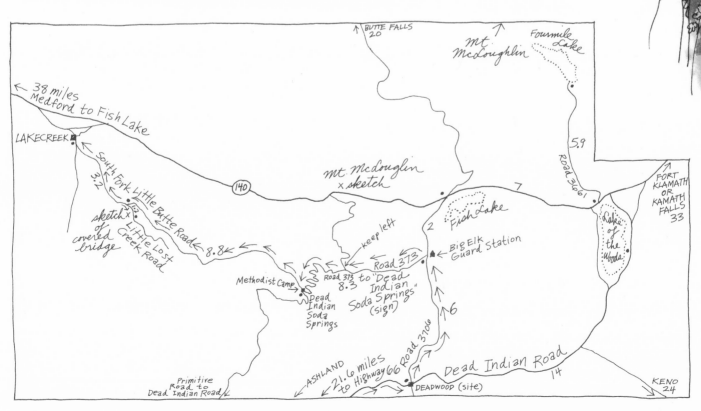

↑ BUTTE FALLS 20

↑ Mt. McLoughlin   Fourmile Lake

← 38 miles Medford to Fish Lake

LAKECREEK

South Fork Little Butte Road 3.2

sketch x of covered bridge Little Lost Creek Road

140

Mt. McDoughlin x sketch

keep left

Road 373

8.8 ←

Road 373 to "Dead Indian Soda Springs" (sign)
8.3

Methodist Camp

Dead Indian Soda Springs

5.9

Road 3661

7

2 Fish Lake

Big Elk Guard Station

6

Lake of the Woods

↑ FORT KLAMATH OR KAMATH FALLS 33

ASHLAND 21.6 miles to Highway 66 Road 3706

Dead Indian Road 14

Primitive Road to Dead Indian Road

DEADWOOD (site)

KENO 24

Little Lost Creek
Covered Bridge

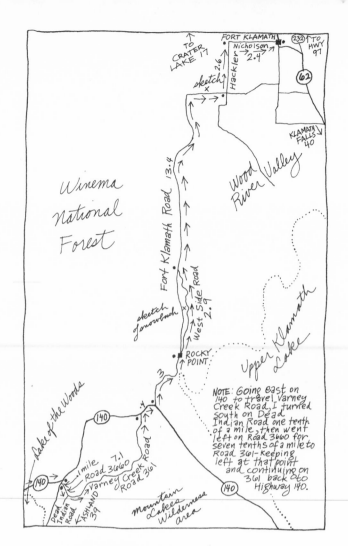

Winema
National
Forest

TO
CRATER
LAKE 17

FORT KLAMATH

232 TO HWY 97

Nicholson 2.4

62

Fort Klamath Road 13.4

Hackler 2.6

sketch
X

KLAMATH FALLS 40

Wood River Valley

sketch of snowbush

West Side Road 2.9

ROCKY POINT

Upper Klamath Lake

3

Lake of the Woods

140

140

1 mile

Road 3660 7.1

Varney Creek Road

Road 361

Dead Indian Road

ASHLAND 39

Mountain Lakes Wilderness area

140

NOTE: Going east on 140 to travel Varney Creek Road, I turned south on Dead Indian Road one tenth of a mile, then went left on Road 3660 for seven tenths of a mile to Road 361-keeping left at that point and continuing on 361 back oto Highway 140.

View from Klamath Meadows

The road to Fort Klamath and the Invisible Mountain

From Lake of the Woods, Varney Creek Road parallels Highway 140, a quiet forest drive. At Rocky Point I turned off the Fort Klamath Road for the slower pace of West Side Road. In June the sweetly fragrant snowbush lined the roadside. Later, crossing Fort Klamath Meadows, I sketched the broad view looking north toward the region of Crater Lake and the now invisible Mt. Mazama, which once dominated this landscape. Indian legend tells of a great eruption and the collapse of the former 15,000-foot Mt. Mazama, a story supported by geologists.

Snowbush

Crater Lake and Grayback
Ridge Motor Nature Trail

Indian legend best describes
Crater Lake to me. The medicine
men of Klamath, who were the
only people the Spirit Chief
allowed to visit the lake, pictured
it as a giant cave... "The cave is
deep and bottomless, as deep
and bottomless as the sky. The
mountains around it sink far
into the earth and reach toward
the clouds. The cave is filled
with blue water--water of a
deeper blue than the sky
which looks at itself in the lake."*
    Grayback Ridge Motor Trail is through a mountain
hemlock, lodgepole pine, and mixed conifer forest.
On my trip chipmunks bounded across the road
and fat black and gray birds, pine nut loving
"Clark's Nutcrackers," were much
in evidence. There were long
views of Matterhorn like
    Union Peak, Mt. McLoughlin,
    Crater Peak and faraway
        Mt. Shasta.

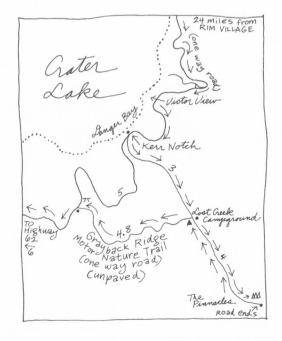

Crater
Lake

↓ 24 miles from
RIM VILLAGE

(one way road)

Victor View

Danger Bay

Kerr Notch

3

5

TT

TO
Highway
62
← 6

4.8

Grayback Ridge
Motor Nature Trail
(one way road)
(unpaved)

Lost Creek
Campground

The
Pinnacles
Road ends

*from Indian Legends of the Pacific Northwest,
by Ella E. Clark; Copyright 1953, The Regents of
the University of California; reprinted by
permission of the University of California Press.

Crater Lake

High bluffs near
Toketee Falls

46

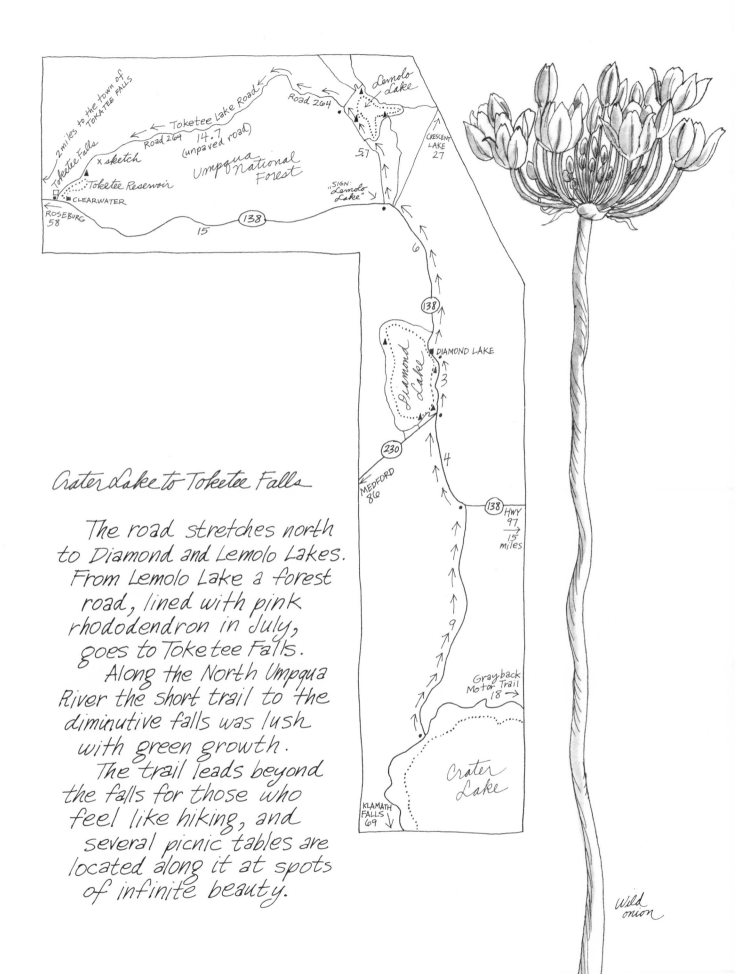

2 miles to the town of TOKATEE FALLS

Toketee Lake Road
Road 264   14.7
(unpaved road)

Road 264

Toketee Falls
X sketch
Toketee Reservoir
CLEARWATER
ROSEBURG 58

Umpqua National Forest

138

15

Road 264

Lemolo Lake

5.7

CRESCENT LAKE 27

"SIGN: Lemolo Lake"

6

138

DIAMOND LAKE

Diamond Lake

3

230

MEDFORD 86

4

138 HWY 97 → 15 miles

9

Grayback Motor Trail 18 →

Crater Lake

KLAMATH FALLS 69

Crater Lake to Toketee Falls

The road stretches north to Diamond and Lemolo Lakes. From Lemolo Lake a forest road, lined with pink rhododendron in July, goes to Toketee Falls.

Along the North Umpqua River the short trail to the diminutive falls was lush with green growth.

The trail leads beyond the falls for those who feel like hiking, and several picnic tables are located along it at spots of infinite beauty.

Wild onion

Tiger Lily

Blackberry

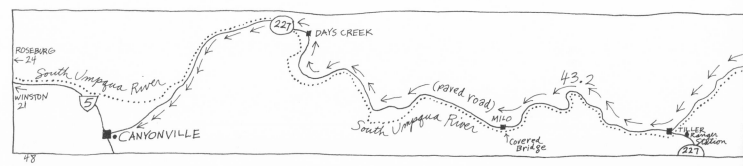

ROSEBURG
← 24

WINSTON
21

South Umpqua River

227 DAYS CREEK

5

CANYONVILLE

(paved road)

South Umpqua River

MILO

↑ Covered
Bridge

43.2

TILLER
Ranger
Station

227

Road to the South Umpqua River

This is a forest drive lined with yarrow, lupine, and elderberry along the roadside. I stopped to draw a brilliant orange tiger lily. At South Umpqua Falls I had a swim before sitting down to draw. Young people were diving and tumbling over the falls, and a group of boys in five truck inner tubes held onto each other as they went over the falls. I had some doubts about their safety, but in the tangle of tubes, bodies, and churning water, they survived with much shouting and laughter.

ROSEBURG 50

CLEARWATER 7.8

138

SIGN: "BIG CAMAS"

× flower sketches

Road 2734

Copeland Creek Road

(unpaved road)

13.5

Road 2734

Rhododendron Ridge

Umpqua National Forest

FRENCH JUNCTION 4800'

Buckhead Mountain

Road 3134

Rolling Grounds Camp

13.5

Black Rock Fork

Deer Lick Falls

Castle Rock Fork

Road 2734

Road 2838

4.4

South Umpqua River

Road 284

× South Umpqua Falls sketch

Campbell Falls

South Umpqua River

Umpqua National Forest

Starflower

49

South Umpqua Falls

51

Brambles in
the window

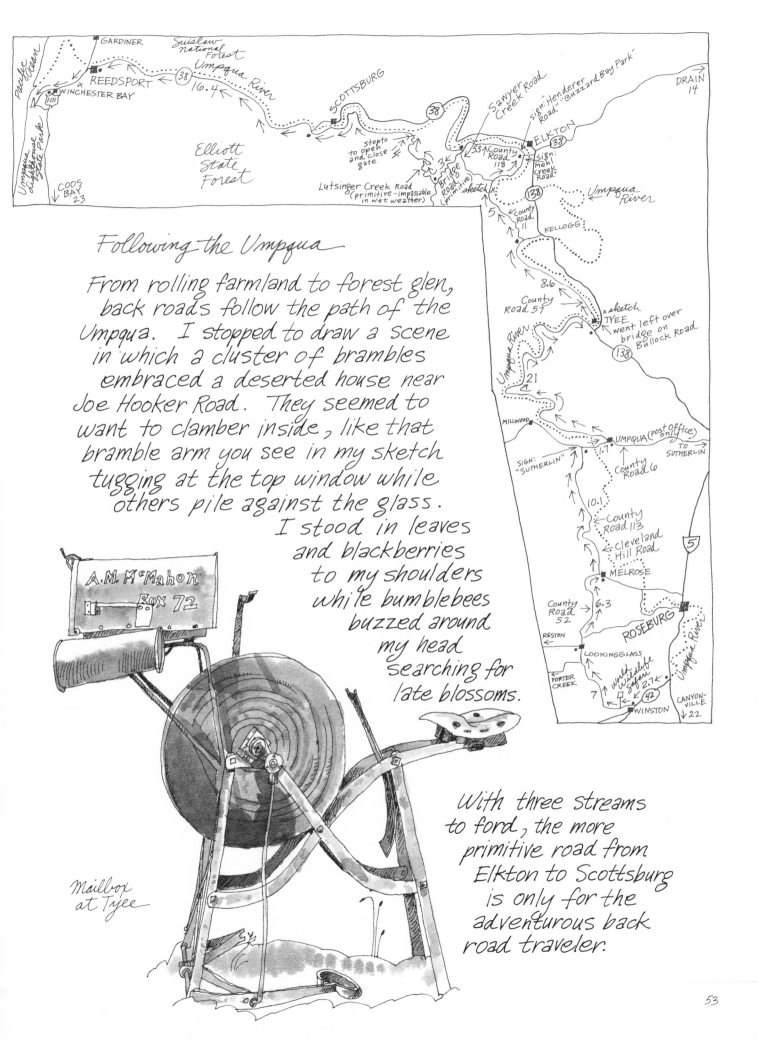

Map labels (top)

GARDINER

Suislaw National Forest

Umpqua River

SCOTTSBURG

Sawyer Creek Road

Sign: Henderer Road "Buzzard Bay Park"

DRAIN 14

Pacific Ocean

REEDSPORT

WINCHESTER BAY

101

(38) 16.4

(38)

ELKTON (38)

5.3 County Road 118

Sign: mehl Creek Road"

Umpqua Lighthouse State Park

↓ COOS BAY 23

Elliott State Forest

stop to open and close gate

2k Bridge Road (primitive)

Lutsinger Creek Road (primitive-impassable in wet weather)

sketch x

(138)

Umpqua River

5

County Road 11

KELLOGG

8.6

County Road 57

x sketch TYEE went left over bridge on Bullock Road

(138)

Umpqua River

21

MILLWOOD

UMPQUA (post office only)

TO SUTHERLIN

.7

County Road 6

SIGN: "SUTHERLIN"

10.1

County Road 113

Cleveland Hill Road

MELROSE

5

County Road 52

6.3

ROSEBURG

Umpqua River

RESTON

LOOKINGGLASS

wild wildlife safari

2.7

7

(42)

WINSTON

PORTER CREEK

CANYON-VILLE

↓ 22

Following the Umpqua

From rolling farmland to forest glen, back roads follow the path of the Umpqua. I stopped to draw a scene in which a cluster of brambles embraced a deserted house near Joe Hooker Road. They seemed to want to clamber inside, like that bramble arm you see in my sketch tugging at the top window while others pile against the glass.

I stood in leaves and blackberries to my shoulders while bumblebees buzzed around my head searching for late blossoms.

A.M. McMahon Box 72

Mailbox at Tyee

With three streams to ford, the more primitive road from Elkton to Scottsburg is only for the adventurous back road traveler.

54

The little road to Umpqua River Lighthouse

    Near Reedsport the Umpqua finally empties into the Pacific Ocean. The nicely proportioned Umpqua River Lighthouse was built in 1892, and its 1,800,000-candlepower light can be seen for twenty miles.

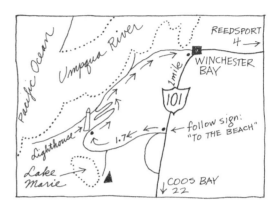

Umpqua River Lighthouse

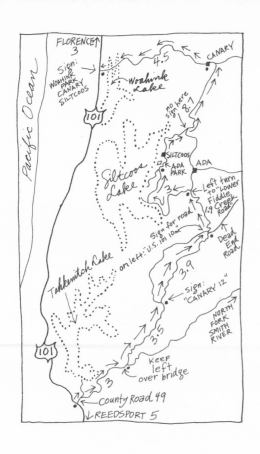

The road to Siltcoos

Here are views of lakes and inlets filled with pond lilies, rushes, old stumps, and ancient mossy logs.
Indians called the yellow-blossomed pond lily I sketched "Wocus," and roasted and ate the large seeds -- if ducks didn't get to them first! Trout prefer the cool water under the pond lilies. To fishermen, the wocus indicates that the water is likely to be too deep for wading in hip boots.

"Wocus,"
Indian pond lily

The Smith River Road to Hadleyville

Green meadows and big barns border the inland riverbank. Tidy houses are tucked into narrow forest canyons on the north side of the road.

The Twin Sisters Campground, a lovely spot shaded by fir trees, was lush and verdant with ferns.

After camping there for the night I sketched a decaying fir stump that nature had adorned with intricate patterns of green growth.

Birdcalls, including the deep-throated cry of the raven, echoed in the cathedral of tall trees.

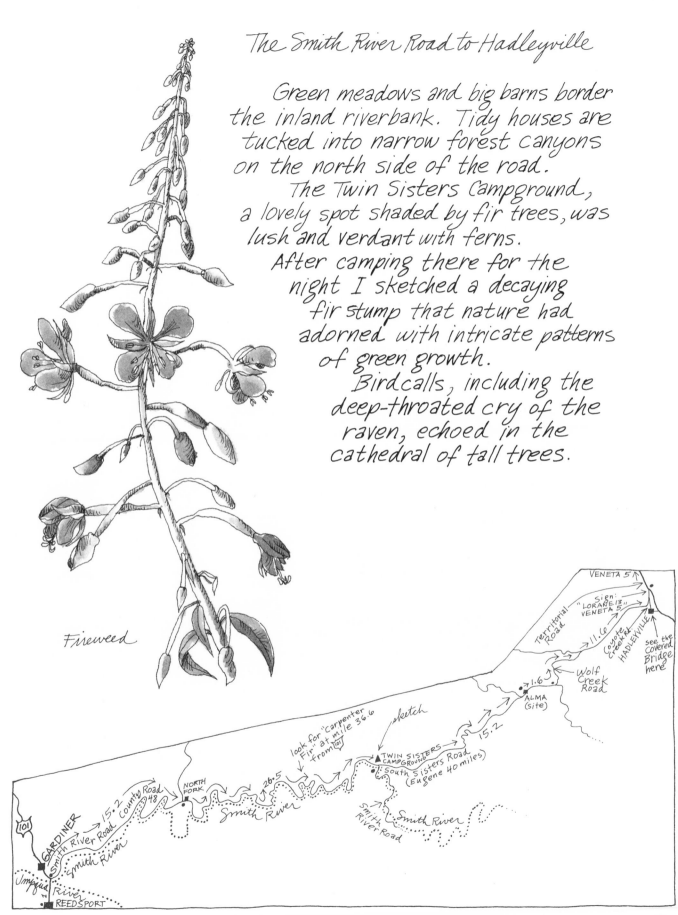

Fireweed

VENETA 5

Sign: "LORANE 13 VENETA 5"

Territorial Road

Coyote Creek Rd. 11.6 HADLEYVILLE

see the Covered Bridge here

1.6 Wolf Creek Road

ALMA (site)

look for "Carpenter Fir" at mile 36.6 from 101

sketch

15.2

TWIN SISTERS CAMPGROUNDS

South Sisters Road (Eugene 40 miles)

26.5

NORTH FORK

Smith River

Smith River Road

Smith River

101

GARDINER

Smith River Road County Road 15.2 48

Smith River

Umpqua River

REEDSPORT

Stump at
Twin Sisters

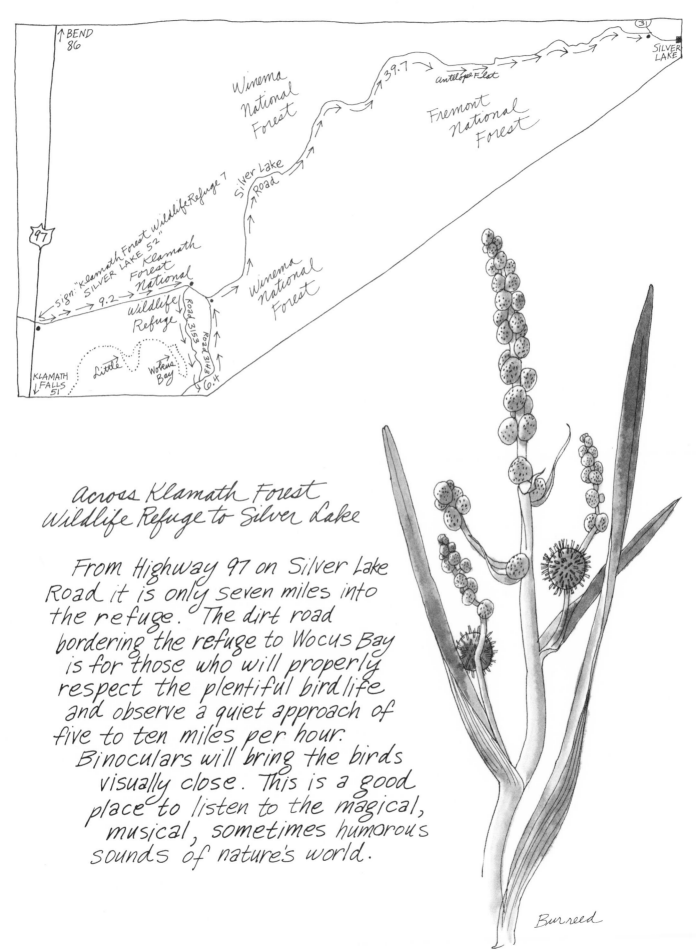

BEND
86

Winema
National
Forest

31
SILVER
LAKE

39.7

Antelope Flat

Fremont
National
Forest

Silver Lake
Road

97

Sign: "Klamath Forest Wildlife Refuge 7"
SILVER LAKE 52"

9.2

Klamath
Forest
National

Wildlife
Refuge

Road 3153

Road 3143

Winema
National
Forest

Winema
National
Forest

KLAMATH
FALLS
51

Little

Wocus
Bay

6.4

Across Klamath Forest
Wildlife Refuge to Silver Lake

From Highway 97 on Silver Lake
Road it is only seven miles into
the refuge. The dirt road
bordering the refuge to Wocus Bay
is for those who will properly
respect the plentiful bird life
and observe a quiet approach of
five to ten miles per hour.
Binoculars will bring the birds
visually close. This is a good
place to listen to the magical,
musical, sometimes humorous
sounds of nature's world.

Burreed

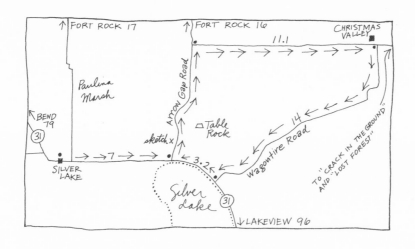

The road from Silver Lake

Arrow Gap Road out of Silver Lake
afforded one of the many views of
distinctive Table Rock. From
any direction it was admirable
in its proportions.

Table Rock

Road to Crack-in-the-Ground

The big crack was not that easy to find, being rather poorly marked. For this reason I have made the mileage count as accurately as possible for you.
There's an interesting variation in temperature from warm to icy as you proceed to walk into the crack. In fact, the interior is so cool that early settlers used to come here for ice when everything else had melted away.
While I was sketching I was startled by a sudden fluttering of wings, and a Red-shafted-Flicker zoomed through the crack, swerving as he narrowly missed my head.
A bit farther on this road you will see lava deposits. Then it is best to return the way you came. I went around the lava flow through miles and miles of sagebrush only generally knowing where I was. With a deteriorating passageway ahead, by luck I was able to find my way back to Christmas Valley.

miles and miles of sagebrush

Crack-in-the-Ground

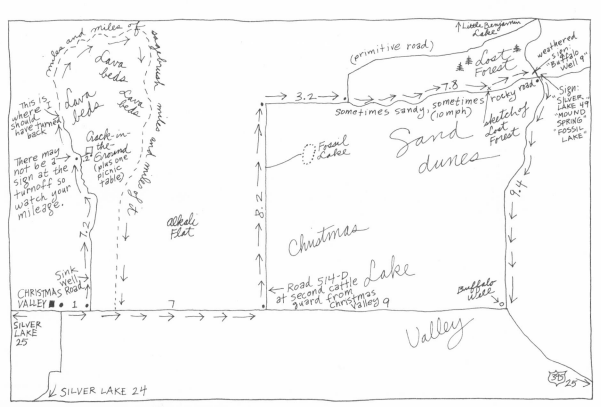

miles and miles of

↗ *Lava beds*

sagebrush miles and miles of

This is where I should have turned back

Lava beds

Lava beds

There may not be a sign at the turnoff so watch your mileage.

Crack-in-the-Ground (plus one picnic table)
.2

7.8

(primitive road)

↑Little Benjamin Lake

🌲🌲 *Lost Forest* 🌲

weathered sign: "Buffalo Well 9"

→ 3.2 →

sometimes sandy, sometimes rocky road (10 mph)

sketch of Lost Forest

Sign: SILVER LAKE 49 "MOUND SPRING" "FOSSIL LAKE"

○ Fossil Lake

Sand dunes

7.2

alkali Flat

20.2

9.4

Christmas

← Road 514-D at second cattle guard from Christmas Valley 9

Lake

Sink Well Road →
CHRISTMAS VALLEY ■ ● 1 ●

7

Valley

Buffalo Well ○

SILVER LAKE 25

↓ SILVER LAKE 24

⑮ 25

64

The Lost Forest

Through the Lost Forest

This is a primitive road and a bit far from
civilization. The trip goes past Fossil Lake, where
important fossils were found in the late 1800s.
The Lost Forest is a unique stand of
ponderosa pine growing forty miles from other
forests in an area so dry that the trees only
receive one-half the rainfall that they would
normally need. Some of the largest junipers
in Oregon also grow here.

Back road from Fort Rock to Hole-in-the-Ground

Fort Rock really is fortresslike, and it is possible to take a somewhat precarious rim drive within the rock's interior. To the west of the rock is a butte enclosing a cave where an archeologist discovered ancient Indian sandals. These were radio-carbon dated at more than 10,000 years, making them the oldest evidence of human habitation in Oregon.

Hole-in-the-Ground, one mile wide, 300 feet deep, was formed by a violent volcanic eruption. The pattern of sagebrush and trees within the hole is striking to contemplate.

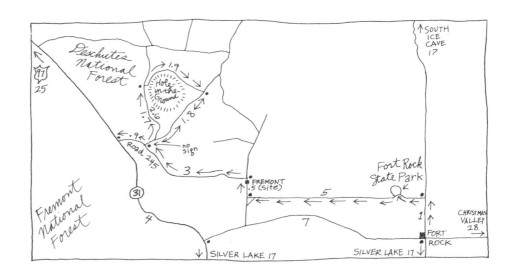

Fort Rock

Paisley to Lakeview

In Paisley I sketched the 100-year-old Tucker place, where Ma Cary, who lived there, kept a large vegetable garden. Flowers were blooming all around the little wooden house.

The old Tucker place

69

Old settler's cabin in the meadow

There were two roads from Paisley into Fremont National Forest. On the high road, in an alpine meadow near Puppy Dog Springs, was this old structure surrounded by grass and wildflowers. On a sunny day in June, when the birds are in strong and sweet voice, it is as good a place to be as anywhere on earth.

71

Juniper

Dog Lake Road to Bly

I must have stayed at Dog Lake's Cinder Hill Camp on the wrong night of the week. The mosquitoes were particularly voracious. However, an old fisherman told me the fishing was good. He had a freezer in his trailer and already had a good stock of fish packed away. Along this forest road I sketched a juniper and a big mule-ears blossom. There were thousands of white pond buttercups on the pond surface at Robinson Spring. A black duck paddled through all the whiteness.

I dripped a blob of black ink on my drawing while striking at a mosquito.

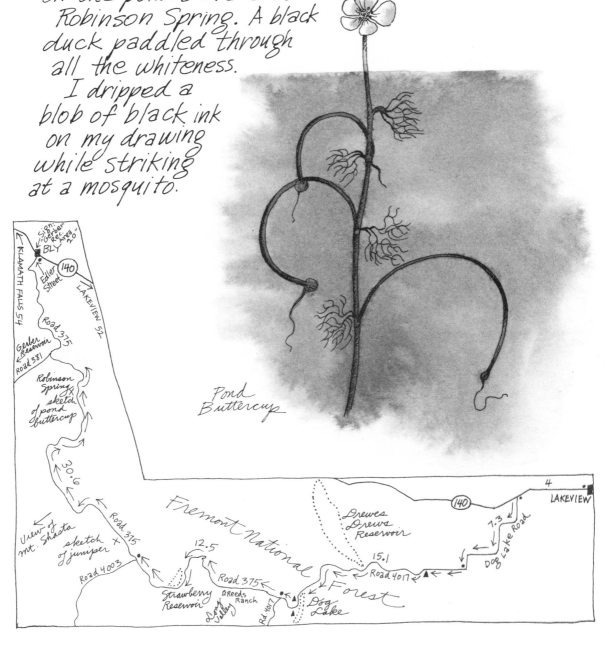

Pond Buttercup

The old Fitzhugh place,
Langell Valley

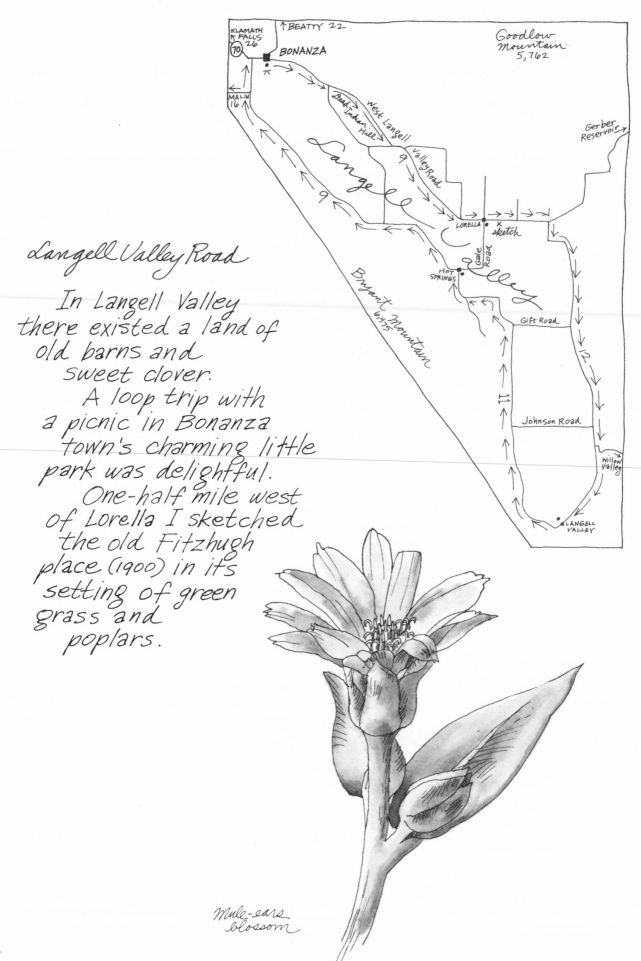

BEATTY 22

KLAMATH
FALLS
26

⑦⓪

BONANZA

MALIN
16

Bush Indian Hill

West Langell

Valley Road

Langell

9

9

Goodlow
Mountain
5,762

Gerber
Reservoir

LORELLA

X
sketch

Gale Road

HOT
SPRINGS

Bryant Mountain
6,475

Valley

Gift Road

11

12

Johnson Road

Willow
Valley

LANGELL
VALLEY

Langell Valley Road

In Langell Valley
there existed a land of
old barns and
sweet clover.
A loop trip with
a picnic in Bonanza
town's charming little
park was delightful.
One-half mile west
of Lorella I sketched
the old Fitzhugh
place (1900) in its
setting of green
grass and
poplars.

Mule-ears
blossom

Round trip through Klamath Basin

There is much drama and many interesting sights along the canals and waterways south of Klamath Falls. Egrets were stationed at intervals along Klamath Strait Drain Outlet, each rising to flight as I traveled slowly down the levee road. Groups of cormorants flew between the dikes, geese scurried to the water to swim to the other side, hawks lay in wait to capture ducklings, and a great white pelican took off into the wind, pushing at the water surface for takeoff speed.

Typical comments by visitors in the Refuge Visitor Register were "Beyond fantastic," "Praise the Lord," "Avocet sounds are super," and my own notation, "Hooray for the birds."

Birds of the Klamath Basin

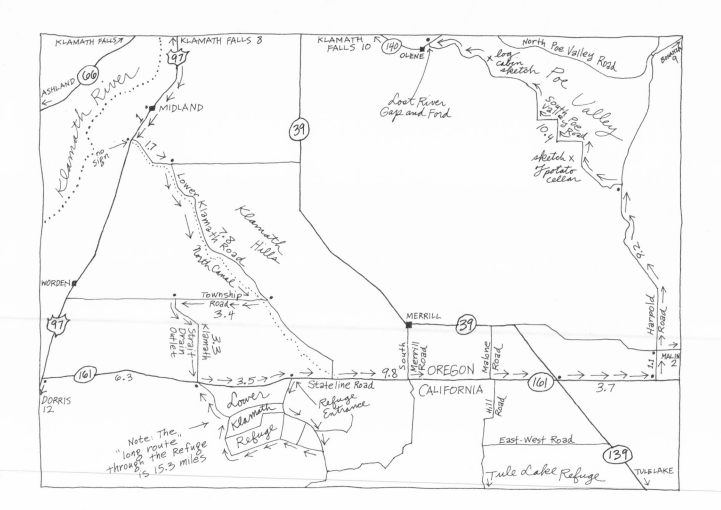

KLAMATH FALLS ↗ ↖ ↗ KLAMATH FALLS 8   KLAMATH FALLS 10   North Poe Valley Road   BONANZA 9

66 ASHLAND   97   Klamath River   140 OLENE   × log cabin sketch   Poe Valley

MIDLAND   Lost River Gap and Ford   South Poe Valley Road 10.4

no sign   1.7   Lower Klamath Road 7.8   39   sketch × ↙ potato cellar

North Canal   Klamath Hills

WORDEN   Township Road 3.4   2.6

97   Strait Drain Outlet   Klamath 3.3   MERRILL   39   Harpold Road   1.1   MALIN 2

161   6.3   ← 3.5 →   9.8   South Merrill Road   OREGON   Malone Road   161   3.7

DORRIS 12   Stateline Road   CALIFORNIA   Hill Road

Note: The "long route" through the Refuge is 15.3 miles   Lower Klamath Refuge   Refuge Entrance   East-West Road   139

Tule Lake Refuge   TULELAKE

Potato Cellar

Within Poe Valley, and indeed in all the farming country hereabouts, are potato cellars. Farmers can store potatoes in these insulated half-barns from September to April.

I drew the trapper's cabin on the site of a
Modoc Indian campground. Sam High originally
purchased the land from the first homesteader
in about 1880. Sam High's grandson told me the
cabin is known to have been there in 1860.
    In returning to Highway 140 on this round
trip through Klamath Basin, a bridge crosses
the Lost River fording place used by the
earliest travelers in this section of Oregon.

Trapper's cabin, circa 1860

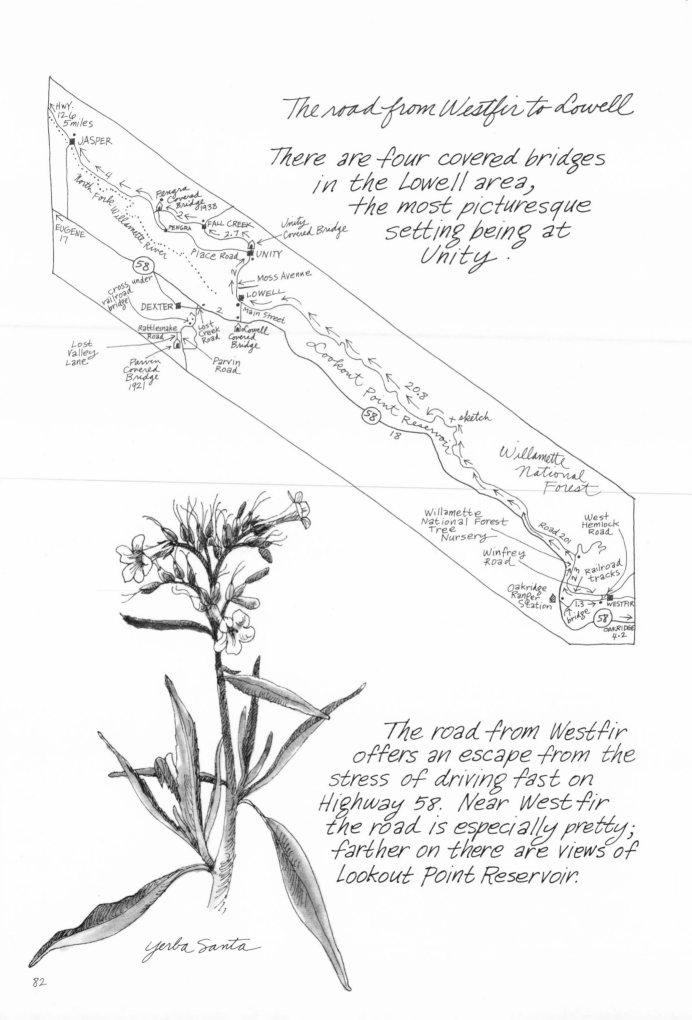

The road from Westfir to Lowell

There are four covered bridges
in the Lowell area,
the most picturesque
setting being at
Unity.

HWY.
126
5 miles

JASPER

← 4

Pengra
Covered
Bridge
1938

North Fork Willamette River

← 2

PENGRA

FALL CREEK

← 2.7

Unity
Covered Bridge

EUGENE
17

Place Road

UNITY

58

Moss Avenne

Cross under
railroad
bridge

DEXTER

← 2

Main Street

LOWELL

Rattlesnake
Road

Lost Creek
Road

Lowell
Covered
Bridge

Lost
Valley
Lane

Parvin
Covered
Bridge
1921

Parvin
Road

Lookout Point Reservoir

20.8

← sketch

58

18

Willamette
National
Forest

Willamette
National Forest
Tree
Nursery

West
Hemlock
Road

Road 201

Winfrey
Road

Railroad
tracks

Oakridge
Ranger
Station

1.3
bridge

WESTFIR

58

OAKRIDGE
4.2

The road from Westfir
offers an escape from the
stress of driving fast on
Highway 58. Near West fir
the road is especially pretty;
farther on there are views of
Lookout Point Reservoir.

yerba Santa

The road
from Westfir

83

Back road of caves and lakes

    The landscape was of pine and sagebrush,
gently rolling across the high desert.
    At Skeleton Cave I sketched by
flashlight in the cool interior.
There was much to see in this volcanic
    area south of Bend.
    With stops at four caves, this
back road took me to Newberry Crater
and its two popular fishing lakes, East
and Paulina. Then there was Lava Cast
Forest, Lava River Caves, and Lava Butte to
visit on the way back to Bend.

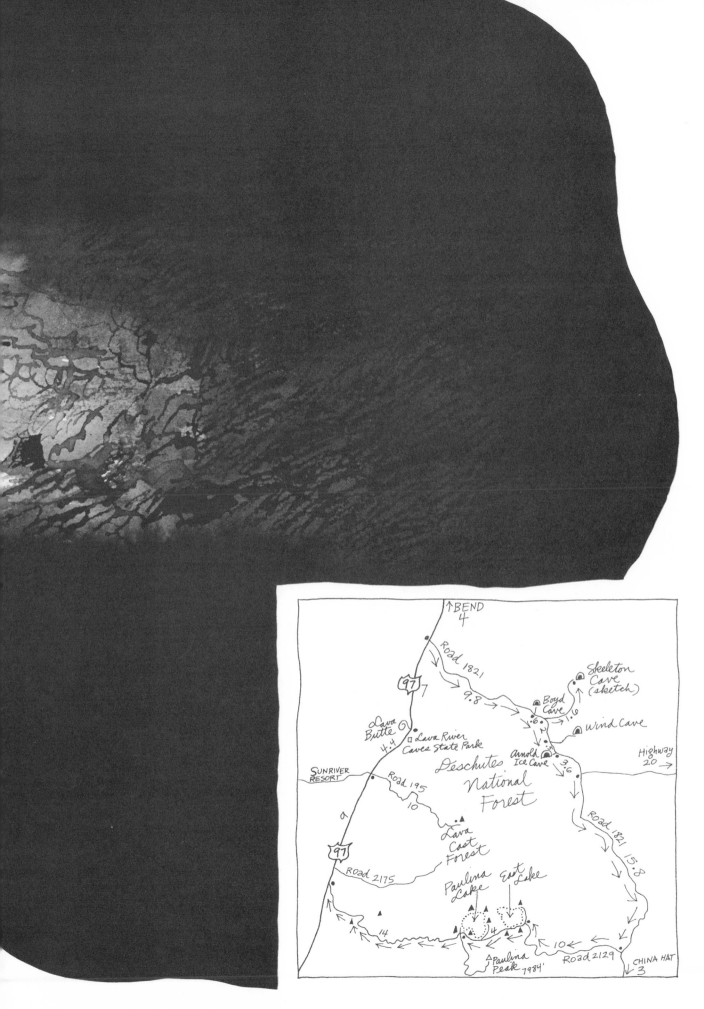

ASTORIA

THE ROAD TO BROWNSMEAD

30

LEVEE ROAD

SIDE ROAD ON PAST MAYGER

THE ROAD THROUGH FORT STEVENS STATE PARK

YOUNG RIVER AND WALLUSKI LOOP, TOO

CANNON BEACH TO ECOLA STATE PARK

26

ST. HELENS

101

ALONG THE MIAMI RIVER TO NEHALEM BAY

SAUVIE ISLAND JOURNEY

6

WASHINGTON

Columbia River

30

Hood River

OREGON

TILLAMOOK

THREE CAPES SCENIC ROUTE

ROADS TO CHURCHES

FOREST GROVE

AND VINEYARDS

PORTLAND

35

26

Following the Nestucca

BEAVER

River to the coast

OREGON CITY ROUNDABOUT TO CANBY

THE SCENIC DRIVE NEAR NESKOWIN

McMINNVILLE

GRAND ISLAND TOUR

CANBY

MEANDERING THROUGH THE WILLAMETTE VALLEY

TYGH VALLEY TO SHERAR'S BRIDGE AND MAUPIN

18

22

SMITH FIELD

5

RIPPLEBROOK TO TIMOTHY LAKE

BAKEOVEN TO SHANIKO

197

FALLS CITY

BASKETT SLOUGH

CITY AND

99E

A HOT SPRINGS TRIP

THE ROAD TO WAPINITIA

97

Pacific Ocean

ELK CITY TO NEWPORT

ALONG THE SILETZ RIVER

101

KINGS VALLEY

THE ROAD TO

RURAL ROUTE TO SALEM

SALEM

THE ROAD TO SILVER CREEK FALLS

THE ROAD TO OLALLIE LAKE

26

SHANIKO

ANTELOPE AND THE ROAD TO ASHWOOD

HOSKINS

THE ROAD TO ELK CITY

20

NEWPORT

ALBANY

22

MADRAS

97

Northwestern Oregon

CORVALLIS

FROM BILLY CHINOOK TO WIZARD FALLS AND THE HEAD OF

THE ROAD PAST STEIN'S PILLAR

26

ALSEA

THE ROAD TO ALSEA FALLS

20

26

MONROE

PEORIA ROAD AND BEYOND

5

ROADS AROUND AND ABOUT BROWNSVILLE

THE METOLIUS

SISTERS

PRINEVILLE

FOLLOWING THE CROOKED RIVER

126

BACK ROAD TO NGST

20

AM THE BLUFFS

REDMOND

126

101

99

Northwestern Oregon

THE OLD TERRITORIAL ROAD

EUGENE

BEND

ANLAUF

Foxglove

Northwestern Oregon

This is a land of enchanting Pacific shoreline, lush green coastal forest, great snowcapped inland mountains, majestic rivers and fertile valleys, and high desert land textured with sagebrush and juniper.

The old Territorial Road

You can travel the old stage road from Anlauf north to Monroe. Along Pheasant Creek it twists and turns as the original road probably did long ago. Farther north it has been smoothed and straightened into a fast highway.

Near Franklin I sketched the Allen barn, erected in 1900, two years before the house was built. A chipmunk sat gnawing an acorn just a few yards from my feet. I included it in the picture.

The Allen barn, 1900

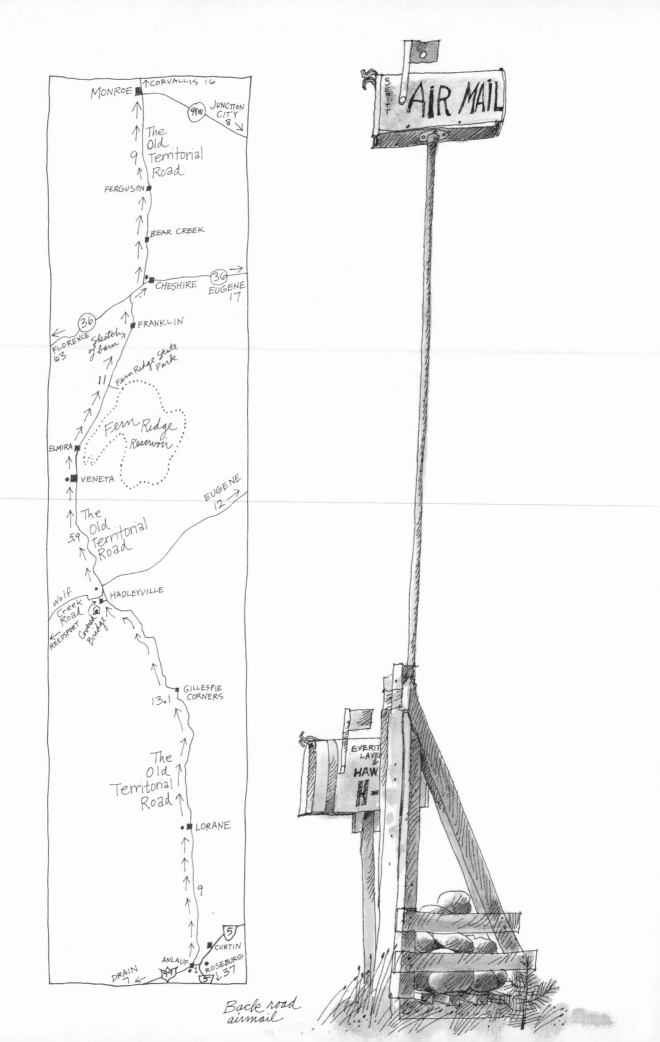

MONROE ↑CORVALLIS 16
(99W) JUNCTION CITY 8

The Old Territorial Road
9

FERGUSON

BEAR CREEK

CHESHIRE   (36)→ EUGENE 17

(36) FLORENCE 63
Sketch of barn
FRANKLIN

11 Fern Ridge State Park

Fern Ridge Reservoir

ELMIRA

VENETA   EUGENE 12

The Old Territorial Road
5.9

Wolf Creek Road   HADLEYVILLE
REEDSPORT← Covered Bridge

13.1   GILLESPIE CORNERS

The Old Territorial Road

LORANE

9

(5) CURTIN

DRAIN ANLAUF (99) ↓ROSEBURG 37

90

Back road airmail

AIR MAIL

EVERIT
LAVE
2
HAW
H-

Back road
mailbox

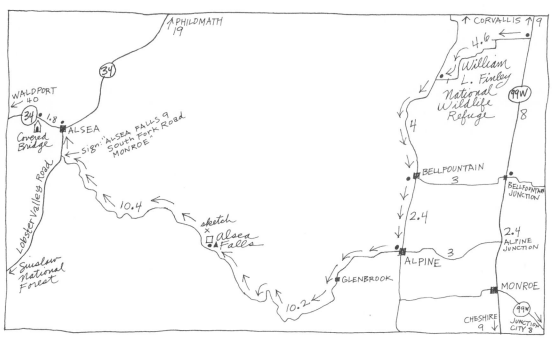

Alsea Falls

92

The road to Alsea Falls

South of Corvallis off Highway 99W this back road begins at the William T. Finley National Refuge. This is farming country, then farther on near the falls, forested land. I camped at Alsea Falls and woke next morning to the sounds and sight of a squirrel chewing a green fir cone to bits. While sketching the falls early that day, I saw thousands of caterpillars inching their way over the rocks next to the Alsea River. I had to be careful where I stepped.

Buena Vista Ferry

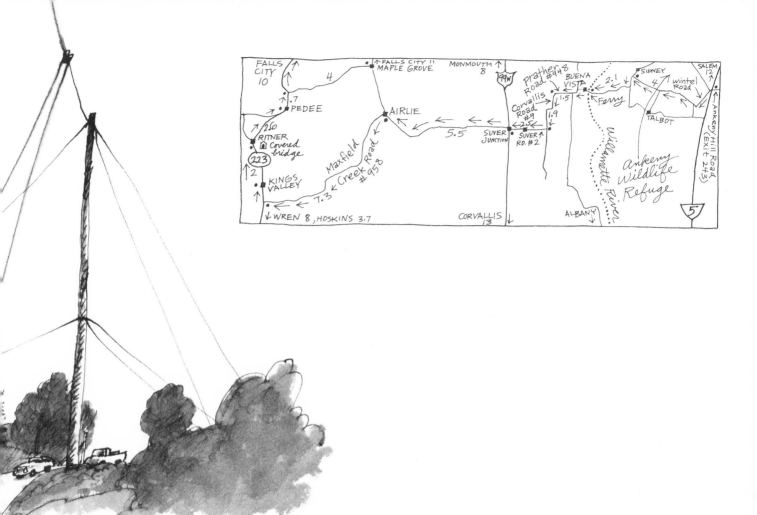

Map labels:
FALLS CITY 10
FALLS CITY 11 MAPLE GROVE
MONMOUTH 8
SALEM 12
4
99W
Prather Road #948
BUENA VISTA
2.1
SIDNEY
4
Wintel Road
.7 PEDEE
Corvallis Road #9
1.5
Ferry
250
RITNER Covered bridge
223
AIRLIE
5.5
1.9
Willamette River
TALBOT
Ankeny Hill Road (EXIT 243)
2
KINGS VALLEY
Maxfield Creek Road #958
SUVER JUNCTION
SUVER RD. #2
2.5
Ankeny Wildlife Refuge
7.3
WREN 8, HOSKINS 3.7
CORVALLIS 13
ALBANY
5

Road to Kings Valley

Crops of corn, wheat,
hops, bush beans, and mint
enrich the scenery on the
road to Buena Vista.
A cool crossing of the
Willamette on the busy
ferry begins a pleasant trip
to Airlie and Kings Valley.

To Falls City and Baskett Slough Wildlife Refuge

At the falls a red-haired, freckle-faced boy
climbed the waterfall, made a sensational leap
clear of the massive rock cliffs to the water
below, then scaled the thirty feet of rock
cliff to receive my congratulations.

Map labels

WILLAMINA 14

AMITY 10

turn right on Smithfield Rd. #752   4.6

22

.2   2.7   Oak Grove Road

Baskett Slough Wildlife Refuge

.7   Oak Grove Road #7411

from Dallas take 223 toward Valley Junction

Bottle Ranch

2.6   POLK STATION

Crowley Road

99W

OAK GROVE (see the old church, 1884)

28

ELLENDALE

223

2.1

Road #20

1.4

DALLAS

22

SALEM 6

OAKDALE

Oakdale Road #20

4.4

FALLS CITY

1   Falls City Road

Clark Road #868

FROST ROAD #860   3.2

#6

2

223

McTimmond's Road

4

223

AIRLIE 6

.7

PEDEE

KINGS VALLEY 4.6

Text

I sketched the old Hollowell House at 3rd and Pine Streets. Deep blue hyacinths accented the freshly painted white exterior.

Just past the hamlet of Ellendale was Bottle Ranch, adorned with astonishing bottle motifs.

Dallas has an interesting block of historic buildings along its main square.

The old Hollowell House

97

The road to Elk City

Elk City is a quiet
hamlet along the Yaquina
River. You can buy worms
at the store and sit on the
pier to fish the quiet river.
Inspired by Elk City's
restfulness, I camped near
the store under a great
Oregon ash tree where there
once had been a sawmill.
I awoke in the morning to find a
huge local setter pointing directly at
me; I guess a stranger in town
was not necessarily to be trusted.
We made friends, however.

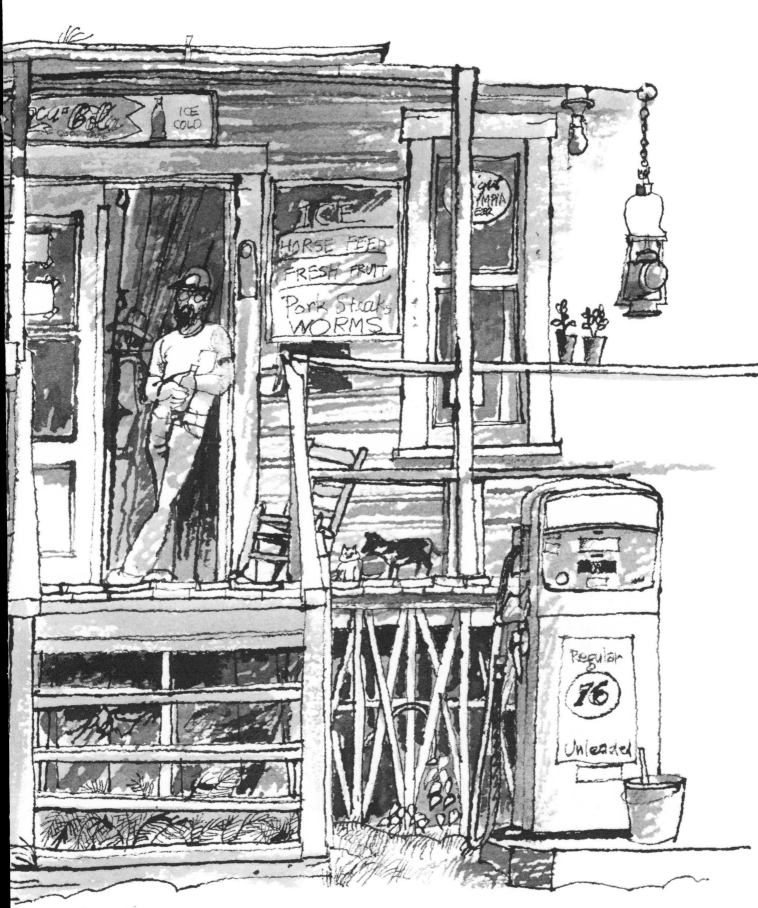

Elk City store

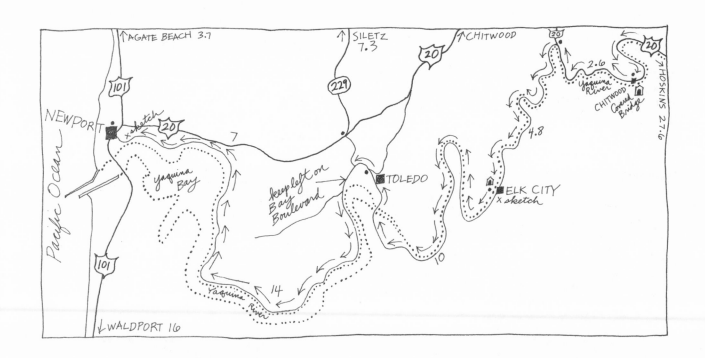

Map labels:
↑ AGATE BEACH 3.7
↑ SILETZ 7.3
↑ CHITWOOD
20
20
20
2.6
Yaquina River
CHITWOOD Covered Bridge
↗ HOSKINS 27.6
101
229
NEWPORT
× sketch
20
Pacific Ocean
Yaquina Bay
keep left on Bay Boulevard
7
TOLEDO
4.8
ELK CITY × sketch
10
14
Yaquina River
101
↓ WALDPORT 16

Elk City to Newport following the Yaquina

The road hugged the shore of the river.
Mist rose from its surface in the early morning.
Hundreds of fishing boats of all kinds were
moored or beached near Newport, and fish
and shellfish could be purchased at a
lively wharf area.

Yaquina Bay fishing boat

100

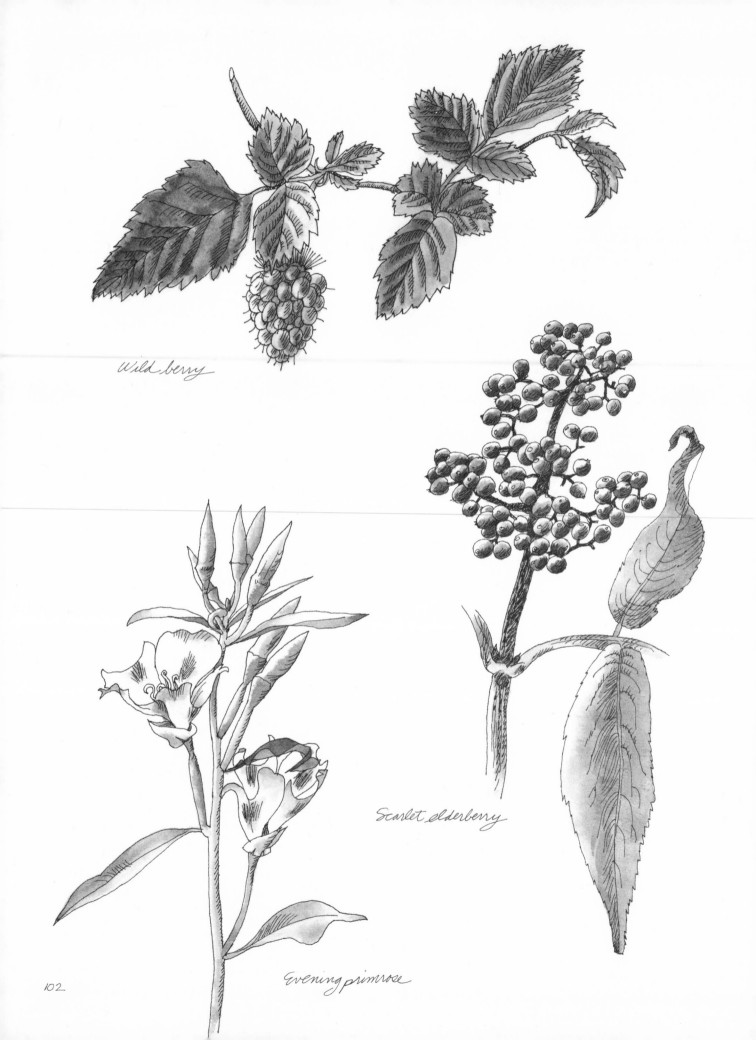

Wild berry

Scarlet elderberry

Evening primrose

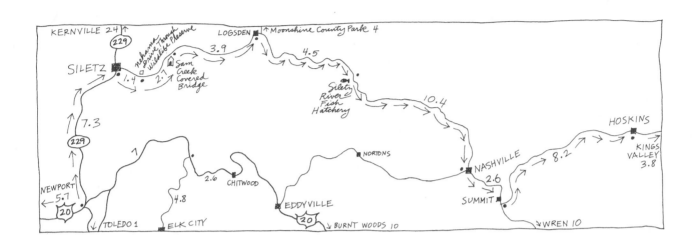

KERNVILLE 24 ↑

229

SILETZ

Nehama Drive Through Wildlife Preserve

Sam Creek Covered Bridge

1.4   2.7

LOGSDEN

↑ Moonshine County Park 4

3.9   4.5

Siletz River Fish Hatchery

10.4

HOSKINS

KINGS VALLEY 3.8

↑ 7.3

229

NORTONS

NASHVILLE

2.6

8.2

NEWPORT
5.7

20

7

2.6   CHITWOOD

4.8

EDDYVILLE

20

SUMMIT

↓ TOLEDO 1   ELK CITY

↓ BURNT WOODS 10

↓ WREN 10

Along the Siletz River to old Fort Hoskins

On this trip there were meadows and barns and forest, a drive through a wildlife preserve and a silver salmon hatchery.
Wildflowers were a continual joy to discover as I sketched.

Back road ruminants

Roundabout to Canby

The Canby Ferry made ten
trips as I sat and sketched
Mr. Hill piloting the
electrically driven
M. J. Lee back and forth
across the Willamette
River. It was a
short but pleasant
trip, and everyone
seemed to enjoy
their brief respite
from car travel.

Note: Turn
off 212 at
12th Street., then,
In 3.5 blocks go
right on Tualatin
Avenue, across the
bridge onto Pete's
Mountain Road.

See the next map:
"meandering
through the
Willamette
Valley"

Canby Ferry

FREE

LIFE PRESERVERS
IN CABIN

EFC 280
M∞OREGON

Canby Ferry ↑1.9 1.6→ East Territorial Road .6
S. Territorial Road ←South Haines Road .6
↑OREGON CITY 6 ←South Beaver Creek Road ↑FISCHERS MILL

1.6 2.8→
South Carus Road 3.4 1.7 ←5
South Bremer Road (views of Mt. Hood) CARUS
South Central Point Road .2

99E BARLOW
Sign: "S LWR HIGHLD RD."
S. Lewellen Rd. .6 HIGHLAND

AURORA 2
LONE ELDER
CLARKES FOUR CORNERS South Meyers Road 1.8 S. Lewellen Road

MULINO
213

South Beaver Creek Road
Windy City Road South Unger Road x sketch of Klæver barn

Note: In all practicality, I could not include all the many roads in this area of the Willamette Valley. Please refer to a Marion County map for complete details. This is an accurate account of my trip, however.

UNION MILLS ←2 3.8 1.2
211 ESTACADA

Rock Creek Church Smyrna Church
1.8 Sconce Road
Gordon Road 2.7 ←S. Dryland Road
211
HAMRICKS CORNER 1.5 2.1 ←S. Cochran Road
MEADOWBROOK
COLTON OLD COLTON

South Barlow Road 2.9
YODER
South Schneider Road 1.5
MOLALLA
CEDARDALE
Feyrer County Park

Darnell-Gibson Road
213
1.3 .3

South Eagan Road
South Kropf Rd.
South Thompson Road
↓KOKEL CORNER
.1
South Lee Road MARQUAM
↓TO Scotts Mills
SCOTTS MILLS

Meandering through the Willamette Valley

The road went through farm and forest land
with a stop to sketch at the Kloer ranch, where
sheep grazed among the stumps.

The Kloer ranch

At Yoder the amiable Walters family ran the neatly kept old Yoder store.
 Not far from here is the 1857 Rock Creek Church set in a historic cemetery. The church is still in use for special occasions.

North Falls

The road to Silver Creek Falls

There are ten falls to see if you hike on all the trails at Silver Creek Falls State Park. One-hundred-thirty-six-foot North Falls is easy to reach via a short trail. One can actually walk around and under the falls to more fully experience its magnificence.

The road to Olallie Lake

This was a rough-surfaced road through high mountain scenery to Olallie Lake. The lake was calm. Voices could be heard clearly for long distances across the water. Mt. Jefferson seemed a bit unreal, like a painted backdrop for a stage setting.

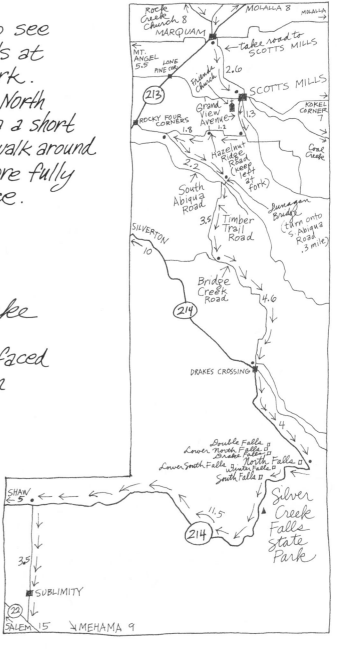

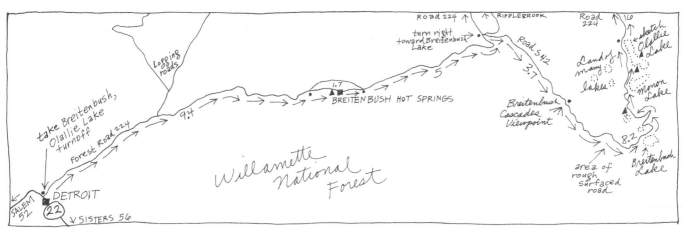

Olallie Lake and Mount Jefferson

A hot springs trip

There were hot springs at Breitenbush, at Austin, and at Bagby. A one-and-one-half-mile trail took me to Bagby Hot Springs. Through the courtesy of Mt. Hood National Forestry Service, there were five separate rooms available for the natural hot baths. Steaming water welled up from the bowels of the earth and flowed past the open window. I pulled the trough bung to fill my big cedar tub, then brought buckets of cold water from the creek to dilute the very hot spring water.

While I soaked in the log tub, thunder rolled and crashed over the Cascades and rain drummed on the roof of the rustic bathhouse -- and I didn't care.

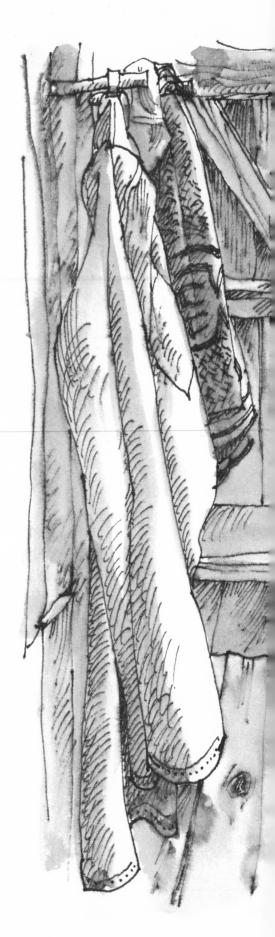

Bagby Hot Springs

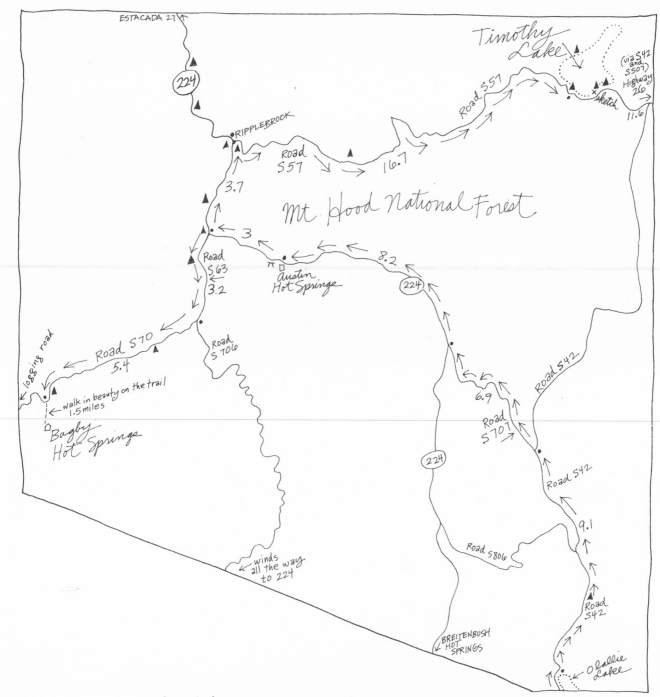

ESTACADA 27

224

RIPPLEBROOK

Road S57

3.7

Road S57   16.7

Mt. Hood National Forest

3

Road S63

3.2

Austin Hot Springs

8.2

224

logging road

Road S70   5.4

Road S706

walk in beauty on the trail 1.5 miles

Bagby Hot Springs

winds all the way to 224

Timothy Lake

(via S42 and S507) Highway 26

11.6

Road S42

6.9

Road S701

224

Road S806

Road S42

9.1

Road S42

BREITENBUSH HOT SPRINGS

Olallie Lake

Ripplebrook to Timothy Lake

Mount Hood is a graceful backdrop
for Timothy Lake. Motorboats
are easily launched on the
lake, which is a popular spot
for families and fishermen.

The road to Wapinitia, Wamic, and Tygh Valley

This is great volcanic plateau land, made even more dramatic by occasional gorges that cut across great areas of landscape.

There was thunder and lightning in the distance and threatening rainclouds gathering overhead. It was 7 PM, and a farmer I passed was desperately threshing the wheat in his fields to get it in before the deluge.

Earlier I sat on Lloyd and Dixie Woodside's porch in Wapinitia and drew at least one-half of the town, with Mount Hood in the background. Wapinitia was a much larger town in the days when wagoneers hauled freight between The Dalles and Prineville That traffic ended many years ago, when the new railroad took over the job.

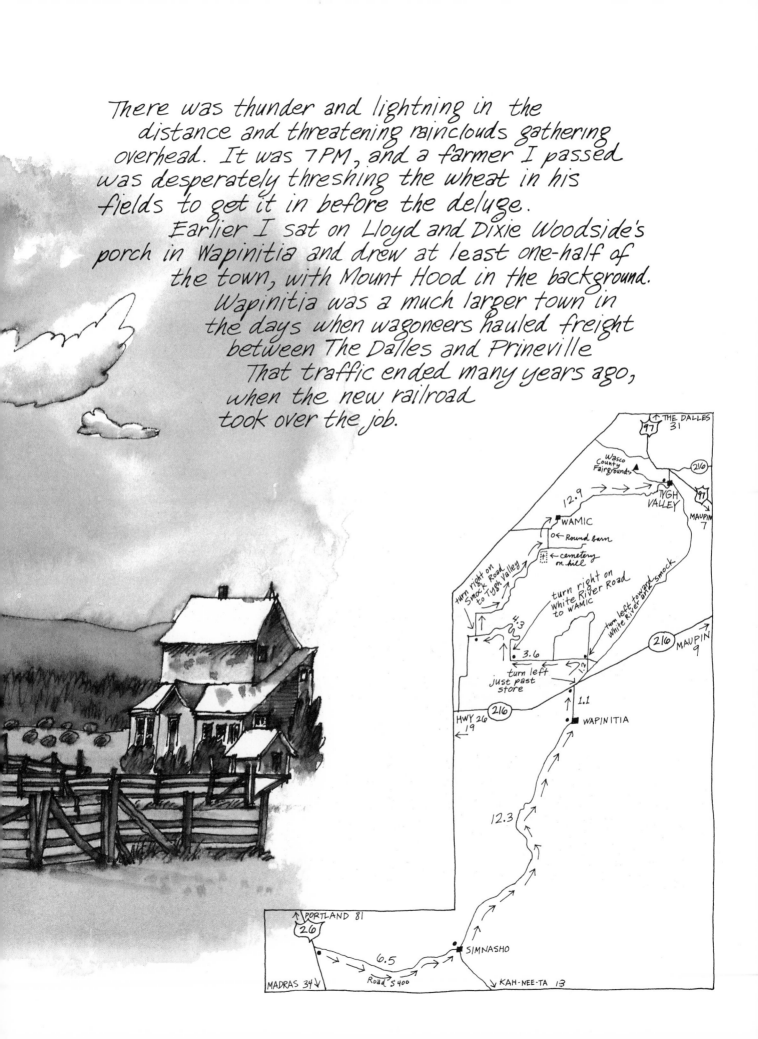

↑ THE DALLES 31
97

Wasco County Fairgrounds
216

12.9
WAMIC
97
TYGH VALLEY
MAUPIN 7

o ← Round Barn

← cemetery on hill

turn right on Smock Road to Tygh Valley

turn right on White River Road to WAMIC

turn left toward White River and Smock

4.3

3.6

216 MAUPIN 9

turn left just past store

1.2

HWY 26 19
216

1.1
WAPINITIA

12.3

↑ PORTLAND 81
26

SIMNASHO

6.5
Road S 400

MADRAS 34 ↓

↓ KAH-NEE-TA 13

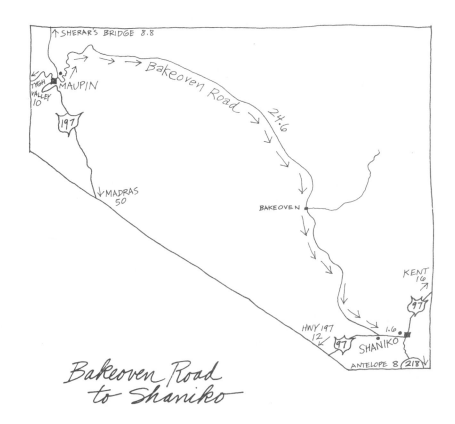

On the map:
↑ SHERAR'S BRIDGE 8.8
TYGH VALLEY 10
MAUPIN
197
Bakeoven Road 24.6
↓ MADRAS 50
BAKEOVEN
KENT 16
97
HWY 197 12
97
SHANIKO 1.6
ANTELOPE 8 / 218

*Bakeoven Road
to Shaniko*

    I don't think the look of
the hotel at Shaniko has changed a great
deal since its beginnings. Once called the
Columbia Southern Hotel, in 1902 the
Shaniko Leader had this to say about it...
"This house is a large two-story brick structure,
finished throughout with the very best of
everything, and is one of the leading hotels
in eastern Oregon. On both floors will be
found hot and cold water, toilet rooms,
bathtubs, etc. It has a fine sewer
connection and no refuse or offensive
matter can pervade the atmosphere, as
is too often noticeable in hotels, especially
in the interior."

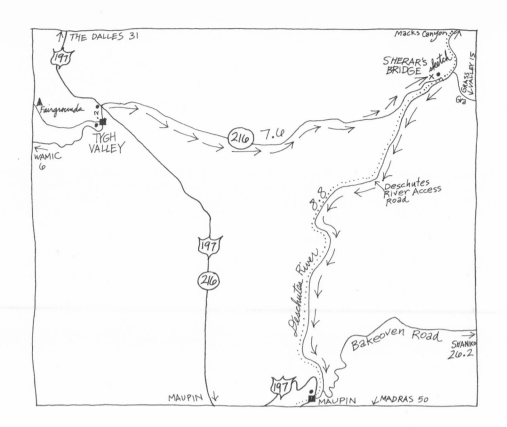

Indians salmon fishing on the Deschutes River

Trygh Valley to Sherar's Bridge and Maupin

Near Sherar's Bridge the ancient Indian trail
led to a place where the rushing Deschutes River
could be forded. The earliest pioneers floated
their wagons across this stretch.
Indians were fishing here the day I sketched.
They tended great nets amid the pounding turmoil
and spray of the river at its frothiest point.

123

Antelope Community Church

Antelope and the road to Ashwood

Antelope seemed a peaceful place.
I sketched the well-preserved Antelope
Community Church to the musical accompaniment
of lawn sprinklers, a crowing rooster, and the
rustling of cottonwood tree leaves overhead.

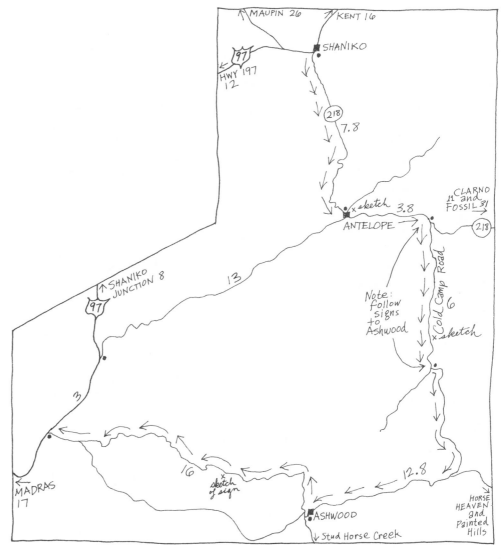

125

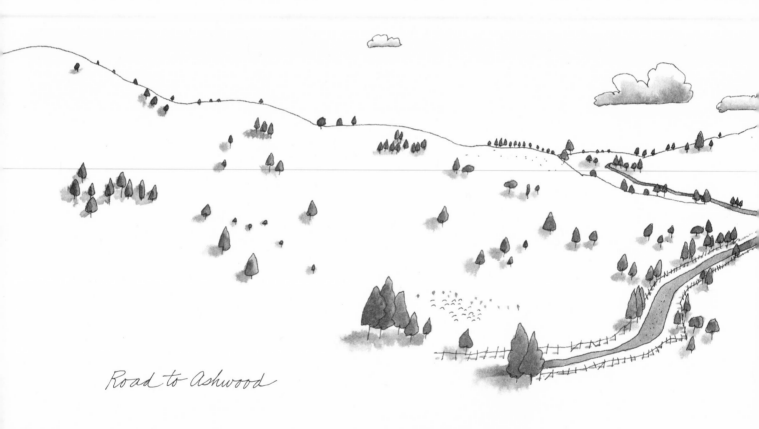

Road to Ashwood

   The store at Ashwood is half-grocery and
half-rock shop, for this is agate and thunderegg
 country. A thunderegg is a rock that is shaped
very roughly like an egg. One must slice it,
however, to see the interesting interior pattern.

At her ranch near Ashwood Mrs. Swanson told me that the sign along the road for attracting rock collectors used to read "Eggs and Agate." Since she has changed the sign to "Agate and Eggs" people do not ask for chicken eggs any longer.

SWANSON AGATE &
EGGS PRESENTS:
CHIEF PAULINA REDS.
VARIETY GOLDS.
BROWNS & BLUES
WITH
PLUME, PRETZEL
POLKA-DOT
+ TUBE DESIGN

OPEN

From Billy Chinook to Wizard Falls
  and the Head of the Metolius

   The air smelled sweet with growing mint around
Madras. I sketched the bluffs at Lake Billy
Chinook to a chorus of doves in the cliffs in back
of me. The road around the lake winds through
rock and juniper.
   At Wizard Falls you will notice the especially
clear quality of the water of the Metolius
River. I sketched a yellow monkey flower
  along the bank while listening to the
   rushing sound of these purest of waters.
     The fish hatchery here is one
     of Oregon's most parklike and
            was a great
             pleasure
              to visit.

Bluffs above Lake Billy Chinook

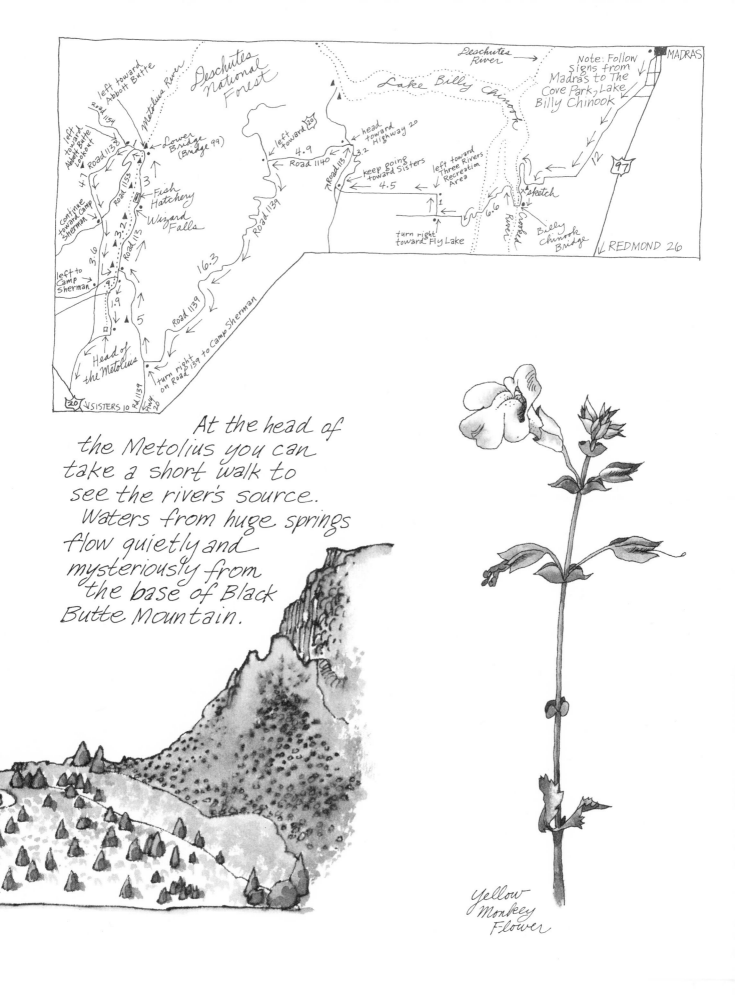

At the head of the Metolius you can take a short walk to see the river's source. Waters from huge springs flow quietly and mysteriously from the base of Black Butte Mountain.

Yellow
Monkey
Flower

Note: Follow Signs from Madras to The Cove Park, Lake Billy Chinook

MADRAS

Deschutes River

Lake Billy Chinook

Deschutes National Forest

Metolius River

left toward Abbott Butte

left toward Abbott Butte Lookout

Road 1154

Road 1138

4.7

Road 1158

continue toward Camp Sherman

3

Lower Bridge (Bridge 99)

Fish Hatchery

Wizard Falls

Road 113

3.2

left toward 20

4.9

Road 1140

Road 113

3.2

head toward Highway 20

keep going toward Sisters

4.5

left toward Three Rivers Recreation Area

sketch

1

6.6

Crooked River

Billy Chinook Bridge

97

12

REDMOND 26

3.6

left to Camp Sherman

9.7

1.9

5

Road 1139

16.3

Road 1139

Head of the Metolius

turn right on Road 139 to Camp Sherman

turn right toward Fly Lake

20

SISTERS 10

Rd. 1139

Hwy. 20

129

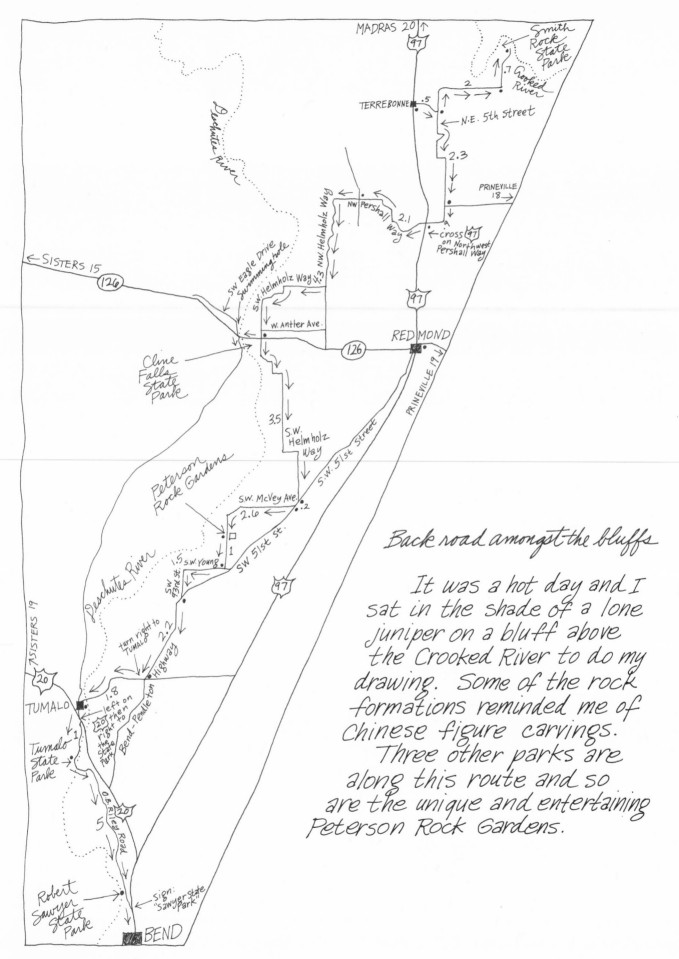

MADRAS 20 ↑
97

Smith Rock State Park

.7 Crooked River

2

TERREBONNE .5

N.E. 5th Street

2.3

PRINEVILLE 18

2.1

NW Pershall Way

cross 97 on Northwest Pershall Way

97

Deschutes River

←SISTERS 15
126

S.W. Eagle Drive
Swimming hole

S.W. Helmholz Way

NW Helmholz Way 4.3

W. Antler Ave.

Cline Falls State Park

126

RED MOND

3.5

S.W. Helmholz Way

S.W. 51st Street

PRINEVILLE 19

Peterson Rock Gardens

S.W. McVey Ave.

2.6 .2

1.5 S.W. Young

S.W. 51st St.

1

SW 93rd St.

97

↗ SISTERS 19

20

turn right to TUMALO

2.2

Bend-Pendleton Highway

.8

left on then right to the State Park

1.8 20

TUMALO

1

Tumalo State Park

0.6 Riley Road

20

5

Robert Sawyer State Park

Sign: "Sawyer State Park"

BEND

Back road amongst the bluffs

It was a hot day and I sat in the shade of a lone juniper on a bluff above the Crooked River to do my drawing. Some of the rock formations reminded me of Chinese figure carvings.

Three other parks are along this route and so are the unique and entertaining Peterson Rock Gardens.

Smith Rock

Stein's Pillar

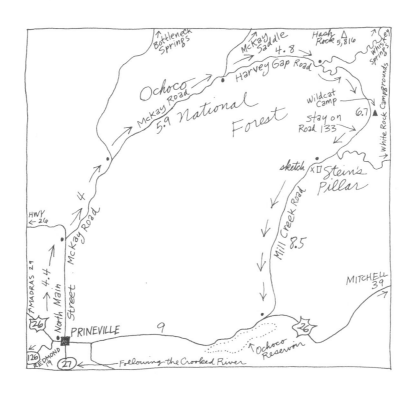

The road past Stein's Pillar

The valley drive past farms and crops soon became forest. On the return journey there was a clear view of Stein's Pillar, a geological oddity towering 350 feet above the floor of the forest.

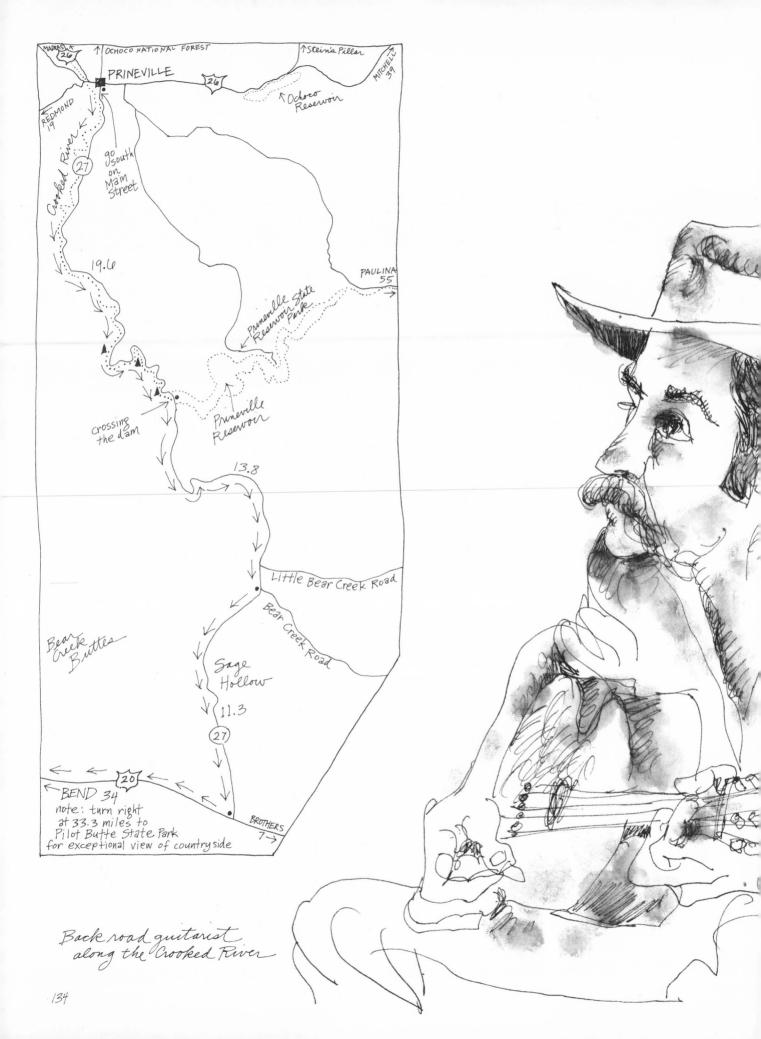

↑MADRAS 26   ↑OCHOCO NATIONAL FOREST   ↑Stein's Pillar   MITCHELL 39

PRINEVILLE   26

↑Ochoco Reservoir

Crooked River   REDMOND 19

27

go south on Main Street

19.6

Prineville State Reservoir Park

PAULINA 55

crossing the dam   Prineville Reservoir

13.8

Little Bear Creek Road

Bear Creek Buttes   Bear Creek Road

Sage Hollow

11.3

27

20   BEND 34
note: turn right
at 33.3 miles to   BROTHERS
Pilot Butte State Park   7→
for exceptional view of countryside

Back road guitarist
along the Crooked River

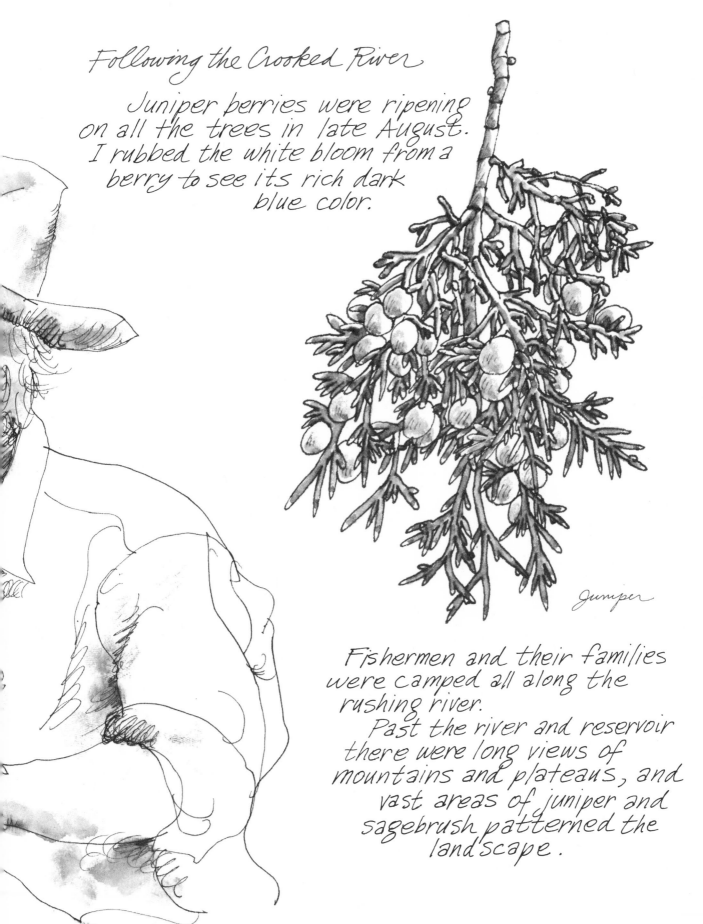

Following the Crooked River

Juniper berries were ripening on all the trees in late August. I rubbed the white bloom from a berry to see its rich dark blue color.

juniper

Fishermen and their families were camped all along the rushing river.

Past the river and reservoir there were long views of mountains and plateaus, and vast areas of juniper and sagebrush patterned the landscape.

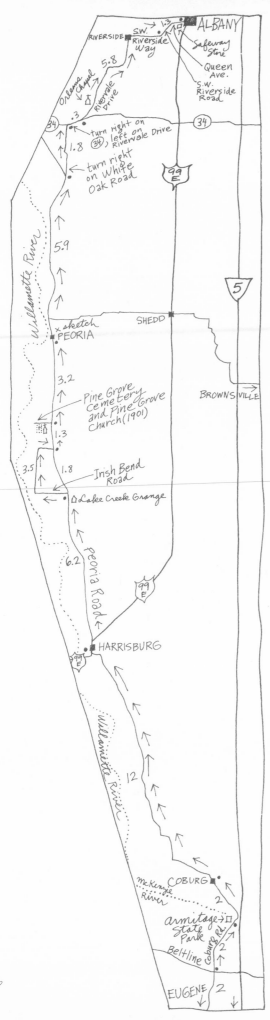

ALBANY

RIVERSIDE

S.W. Riverside Way

Orleans Chapel

5.8

Riverale Drive

Safeway Store

Queen Ave.

S.W. Riverside Road

(34)

.3

(34)

turn right on (34), left on Riverale Drive

1.8

turn right on White Oak Road

99 E

5.9

Willamette River

SHEDD

5

x sketch
PEORIA

3.2

Pine Grove Cemetery and Pine Grove Church (1901)

BROWNSVILLE

1.3

1.8

Irish Bend Road

3.5

□ Lake Creek Grange

6.2

Peoria Road →

99 E

HARRISBURG

99 E

Willamette River

12

McKenzie River

COBURG

2

armitage → □
State Park

Coburg Rd.

2

Beltline

EUGENE 2

Peoria Road and beyond

This road followed the east bank of the Willamette River past well-kept farms and sweet-smelling fields of mint and clover. I sketched at the drowsy hamlet of Peoria where the General Store sells worms.

Peoria General Store

Roads around and about Brownsville

I sat in the shade of a tree that was heavily
decorated with pears to sketch the Blair
Hop-curing House. Along with other
historic buildings in Brownsville (such as
the well-restored Moyer House), it gave
me a feeling for times past.

Blair Hop-curing House

This trip meanders along the Calapooia River, offering views of farms and forest landscapes, and opportunities to explore out-of-the-way places. In Brownsville, where residents sit on their front porches of a pleasant evening, there must have been mild speculation as to who was this tourist driving slowly down their street. It would have been better to walk. Then there is more of a chance for a friendly greeting.

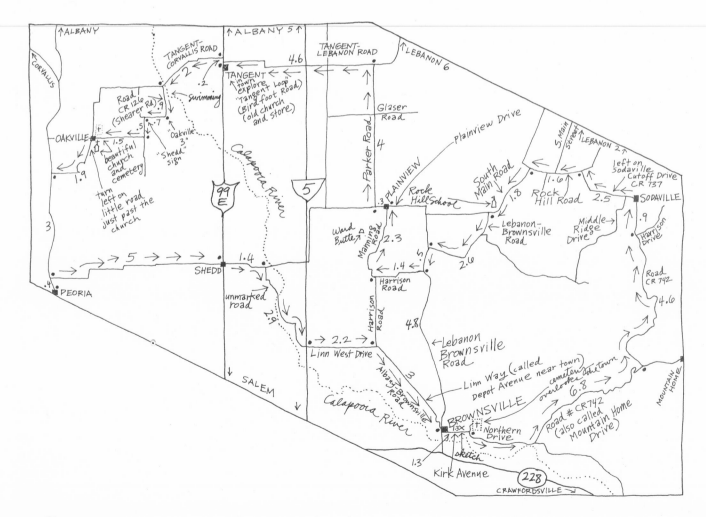

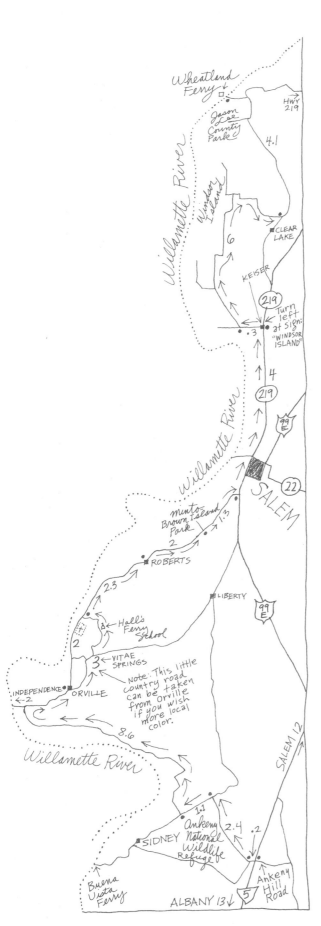

Wheatland Ferry ⌑

Jason Lee County Park

HWY 219

4.1

Willamette River

Windsor Island

6

CLEAR LAKE

KEISER

219

Turn left at sign: "WINDSOR ISLAND"

3

4

219

99 E

Willamette River

SALEM

22

Minto Brown Island Park

1.5

2

ROBERTS

2.3

LIBERTY

99 E

⌂ Hall's Ferry School

2

3 ←VITAE SPRINGS

Note: This little country road can be taken from Orville if you wish more local color.

INDEPENDENCE ← -2

ORVILLE

8.6

SALEM 12

Willamette River

1.1

Ankeny National Wildlife Refuge

2.4

.2

SIDNEY

Buena Vista Ferry

ALBANY 13 ↓

5

Ankeny Hill Road

Hops

Rural route to Salem and the Wheatland Ferry

Still following the Willamette north, I was entertained by the view of fertile farm country and the smell of freshly cut crops. Once I stopped to admire fields of decorative, twining hop vines. I sketched some of the green hop cones and leaves. Ripened and dried, these cones impart a pleasant, somewhat bitter flavor to malt liquors.

141

UNIONVALE

DAYTON·
6.6

McMINNVILLE

14

GRAND ISLAND JUNCTION

1.3

2

FOUR CORNERS

x sketch
Grand Island

3.8

221 2.2

Willamette River

PINE TREE CORNER

HOPEWELL

Maud Williamson State Park

1.1

WHEATLAND

☐ Wheatland Ferry

SALEM↓ 12

Smitty's Produce,
Grand Island

Grand Island tour

There were so many sprinklers going
as I drove along one stretch of this
bucolic farm road around Grand Island
that I needed to keep my windshield
wipers working and windows closed.
At Smitty's roadside vegetable
stand, Snoopy, the dog, ate
a large portion of yellow
wax stringbeans as
I sketched. Here's
hoping Smitty's
is still there.

U-Pick
OPEN
U-Pick
BEANS
PICKLES

BEANS
ONIONS
TODAY
OPEN

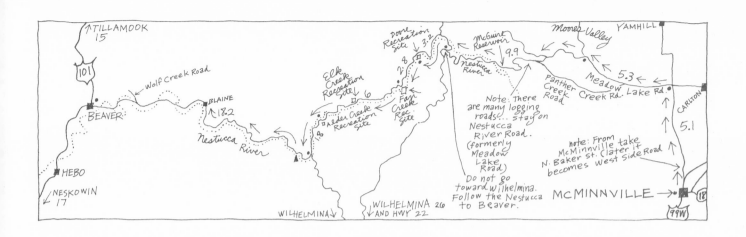

(Map annotations, roughly counterclockwise:)

↑TILLAMOOK 15

[101]

← Wolf Creek Road

■ BLAINE

↑18.2

BEAVER

Nestucca River

■ HEBO

↙NESKOWIN 17

WILHELMINA↓

Doore Recreation Site ↓3.2

8

Elk Creek Recreation Site

Alder Creek Recreation Site □6

1.8

Fan Creek Rec Site □ ←

WILHELMINA 26 AND HWY 22 ↓

↙ McGuire Reservoir

Nestucca River

9.9

Note: There are many logging roads... stay on Nestucca River Road. (formerly Meadow Lake Road)

Do not go toward Wilhelmina. Follow the Nestucca to Beaver.

Moores Valley

YAMHILL ■

Panther Creek Road

Meadow Lake Rd. 5.3 ←

CARLTON 5.1 ↑

note: From McMinnville take N. Baker St. Clater it becomes West Side Road ↑

MCMINNVILLE → ■ [18]

[99W]

Following the Nestucca River to the coast

Leaving the Carlton area there were long views of valleys and farms and big barns. Past the grand panorama of Moore's Valley I headed for the green forests of the Siuslaw National Forest. The road along the Nestucca River led to the town of Beaver.

Cows and redwood tree stumps near Beaver

Oregon morning glory

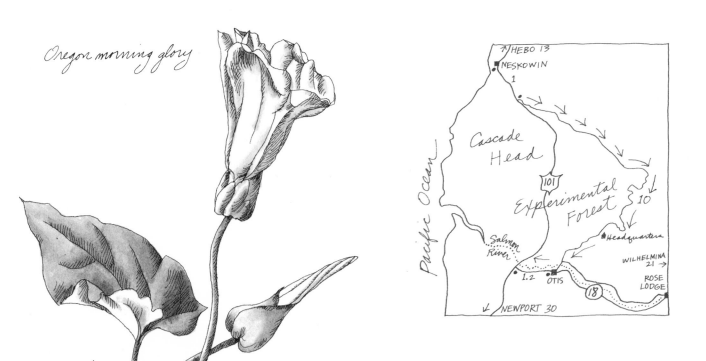

The scenic drive near Neskowin

This was a trip through Cascade Head Experimental Forest, where research is conducted on the management of Oregon's forest reserves.

I sketched a large morning glory blooming creamy white among berry bushes along the road.

Three Capes scenic route

At Cape Kiwanda dories on boat trailers awaited their silver-salmon-fishing owners in a storage lot near the beach. Some trailers had rusty old trucks and cars attached to them ready to go, that is, if the aged vehicles could be started. The dories are flat bottomed and are launched from the beach at Kiwanda. The one I selected to sketch was named Dumship.

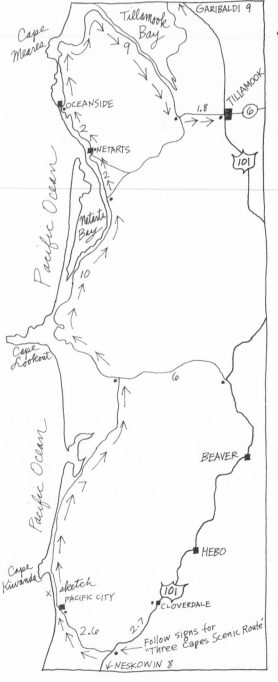

Cape Meares

Tillamook Bay

GARIBALDI 9

9

OCEANSIDE

1.8

TILLAMOOK

6

101

NETARTS

2

Pacific Ocean

2

Netarts Bay

10

Cape Lookout

6

Pacific Ocean

7

BEAVER

HEBO

101

Cape Kiwanda

sketch

PACIFIC CITY

CLOVERDALE

2.6

2.7

Follow signs for "Three Capes Scenic Route"

↓ NESKOWIN 8

146

OR-450

Dumship, Cape Kiwanda

The entire trip was a delight of grand coastal scenery. As I rounded the shores of Tillamook Bay herons were poised in the shallow water, prepared to select any fishy bit that might venture by.

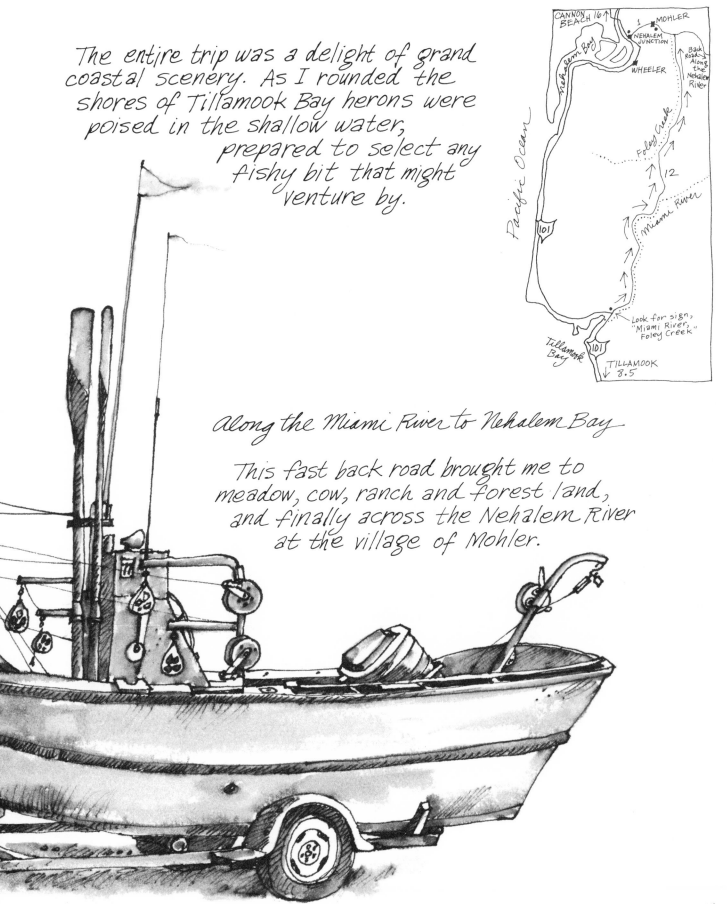

Along the Miami River to Nehalem Bay

This fast back road brought me to meadow, cow, ranch and forest land, and finally across the Nehalem River at the village of Mohler.

Cannon Beach to Ecola State Park

I was at work sketching very early in the morning. Birds flocked around Haystack Rock, their cries mingling with the sound of the ocean waves tumbling on the sand. The scene was intriguing to both ear and eye. Later at the overlook point in Ecola Park I marveled at the beauty of the Oregon coastline.

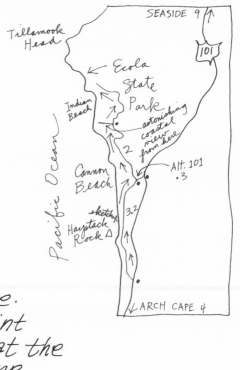

Haystack Rock

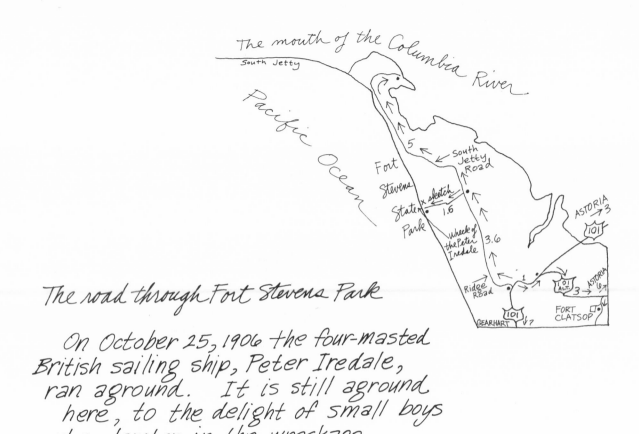

The mouth of the Columbia River

South Jetty

Pacific Ocean

Fort Stevens State Park

South Jetty Road

5

x sketch
1.6

Wreck of the Peter Iredale

3.6

Ridge Road

1

ASTORIA 3

101

101 ALT. 3

ASTORIA 6

GEARHART

101

FORT CLATSOP

7

The road through Fort Stevens Park

On October 25, 1906 the four-masted
British sailing ship, Peter Iredale,
ran aground.   It is still aground
 here, to the delight of small boys
who clamber in the wreckage.
    I drove clear to the end of South Jetty Road
for a view of the mouth of the Columbia River
and the shoreline of the state of Washington.
     The re-creation of Lewis and Clark's winter
headquarters at Fort Clatsop was the
           next thing to see.

The wreck of the Peter Iredale

Young's River Loop
and Walluski Loop, too

Along Young's River I made
a picture of an old barn,
now minus its silo, but still
in use and appreciated by
both cows and artists alike.
    I stopped to view
Young's River Falls. A number
of cars were parked nearby
and I discovered their occupants
swimming and splashing at the
base of the roaring falls.
    The Walluski Loop drive was
a visual feast of farm and barn,
stream and slough.

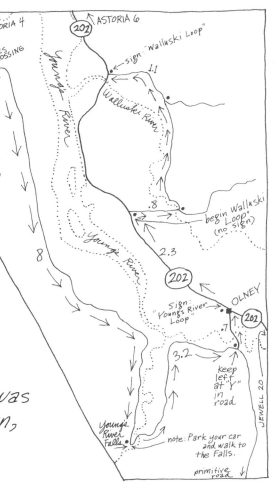

Young's River

Buttercup

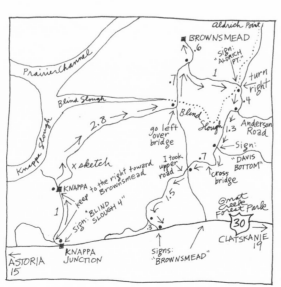

Prairie Channel

Blind Slough

Knappa Slough

2.8 →

Aldrich Point

■ BROWNSMEAD

.6

Sign: "ALDRICH PT."

.7

1

turn right

.4

Blind Slough

go left over bridge

1.3

Anderson Road

x sketch

keep to the right toward Brownsmead

I took upper road

.7

cross bridge

Sign: "DAVIS BOTTOM"

■ KNAPPA

1

Sign: "BLIND SLOUGH 4"

1.5

.3

Gnat Creek Forest Park

30

CLATSKANIE 19

■ KNAPPA JUNCTION

Signs: "BROWNSMEAD"

← ASTORIA 15

Bob Ziak's sign
near Brownsmead

The road to Brownsmead

While I was drawing this scene, Mr. Ziak came by in his tractor. When he realized I was sketching his Canadian goose nest, woodduck house, and sign, he marched, hammer in hand, to nail up the last part of his message, which had fallen down. The complete sign then read, "This land dedicated to the song of birds, the sound of wings to all of nature's creatures, for the joy their presence brings. No hunting. Bob Ziak." It was the gentlest exhortation not to hunt on private property that I had ever seen.

This was a lovely area of waterways and meadows for me to enjoy.

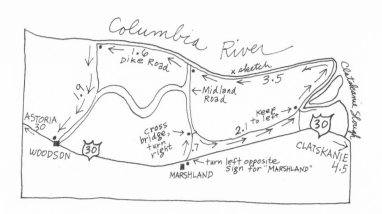

Columbia River

1.6
dike Road

x sketch
3.5

←Midland
Road

Clatskanie Slough

1.9

ASTORIA
30

keep
to left

30

WOODSON   30

cross
bridge,
turn
right

2.1

CLATSKANIE
4.5

.7

←turn left opposite
sign for "MARSHLAND"

MARSHLAND

Levee back road along the Columbia

Trees seem to grow out of old pilings
in the Columbia River. I saw a great
many that day.
    The Columbia River retains its
        majesty even though man has it pretty
    well under control. At several points I had
the feeling I was seeing the great river
    as it was in Lewis and Clark's day, until
an oil tanker would slip around the bend.

The Columbia River

Side road past Mayger on the Columbia

    On Depot Street, just off the road to
Mayger, I sketched the Clatskanie Depot.
I was hoping a train would come
by, but there was no such luck.
    At Mayger Downing Church I ate lunch
and inspected headstones in the
       the graveyard.

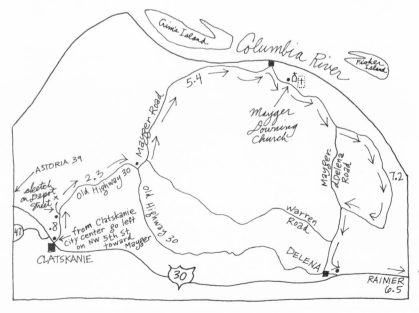

The old depot

159

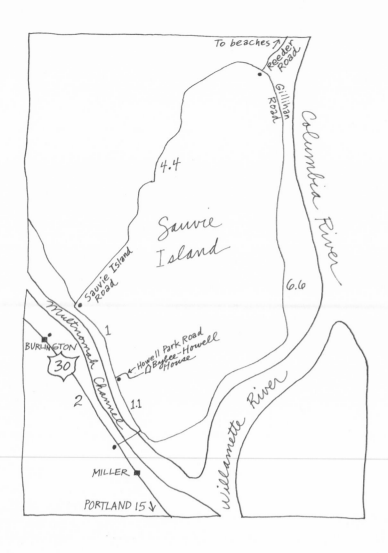

Sauvie Island journey

　　　I stopped to visit the Bybee-Howell house
while traveling around Sauvie Island. It was
named after two families that had lived there
since it was built in 1856. This historic house
is presently maintained by the Oregon Historical
Society for Multnomah County and is open to
the public. The 1860 doll looking at you in my
picture was sitting in a rocking chair in one
of the upper rooms.
　　　I passed many vegetable farms and paused
at the popular beaches along the Columbia River.

The doll,
1860

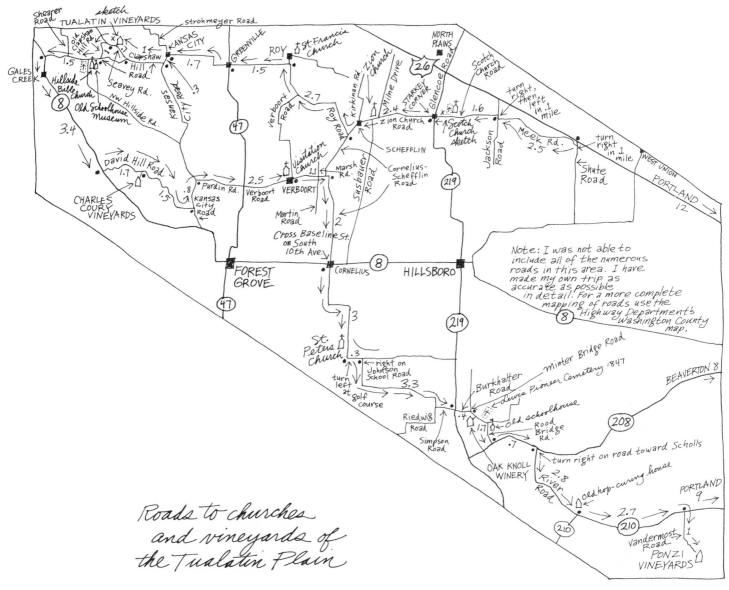

Roads to churches
and vineyards of
the Tualatin Plain

Certainly one of the most
eye-catching of the Oregon churches
I saw during my travels was
The Old Scotch Church.
I tried to approximate the charm
of its setting of tall trees and
green-lawned cemetery
in this drawing.
At Roy I found another striking
church with a silver tower shining
in the sun.

The Old Scotch Church

163

164

I tasted one of winemaker Bill Fuller's excellent rieslings at Tualatin Vineyards. To mark the occasion I sketched this view from the vineyard of young vines to the Tualatin plain in the distance.

These back roads took me to four wineries in all (they are usually open to visitors on weekends) and past views of many fine churches along the way.

At the Dutch community of Verboordt the handsome Catholic church was surrounded by colossal redwood trees.

Tualatin Vineyards

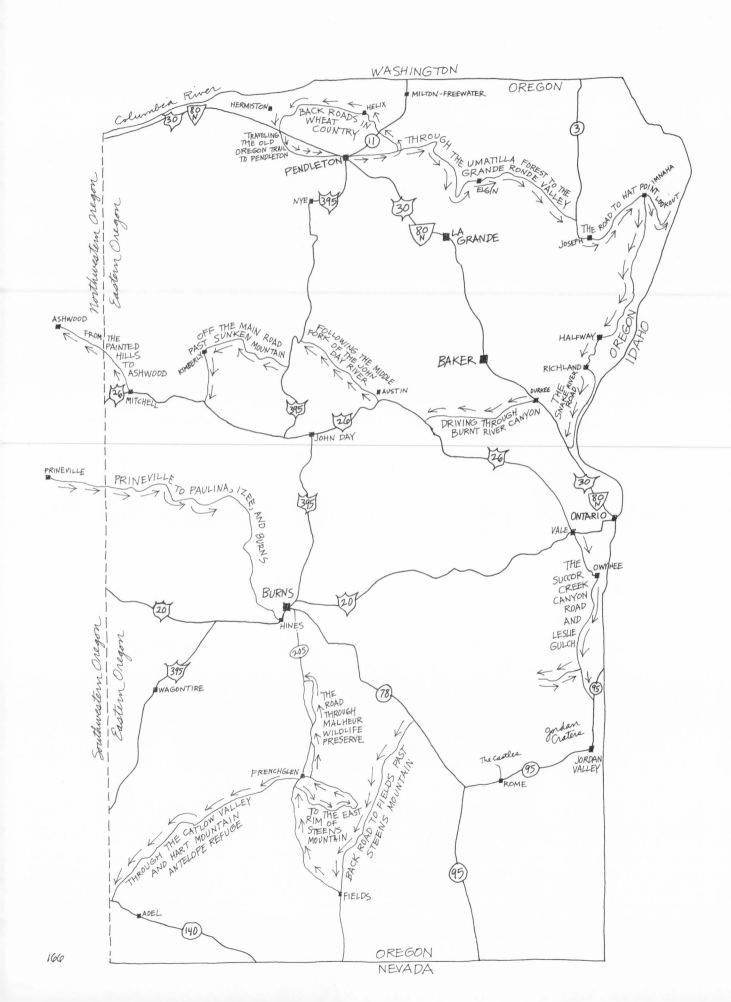

WASHINGTON

OREGON

Columbia River

MILTON-FREEWATER

30 / 80 N

HERMISTON

HELIX

BACK ROADS IN WHEAT COUNTRY

TRAVELING THE OLD OREGON TRAIL TO PENDLETON

11

PENDLETON

THROUGH THE UMATILLA FOREST TO THE GRANDE RONDE VALLEY

3

ELGIN

THE ROAD TO HAT POINT / IMNAHA

NYE

395

30

JOSEPH

80 N

LA GRANDE

LOOKOUT

HALFWAY

OREGON

IDAHO

ASHWOOD

FROM THE PAINTED HILLS TO ASHWOOD

OFF THE MAIN ROAD PAST SUNKEN MOUNTAIN

FOLLOWING THE MIDDLE FORK OF THE JOHN DAY RIVER

BAKER

RICHLAND

KIMBERLY

AUSTIN

DURKEE

THE SNAKE RIVER ROAD

26

MITCHELL

395

26

DRIVING THROUGH BURNT RIVER CANYON

JOHN DAY

26

PRINEVILLE

PRINEVILLE TO PAULINA, IZEE, AND BURNS

395

30

80 N

ONTARIO

VALE

OWYHEE

THE SUCCOR CREEK CANYON ROAD AND LESLIE GULCH

BURNS

20

20

HINES

205

395

WAGONTIRE

78

THE ROAD THROUGH MALHEUR WILDLIFE PRESERVE

95

Jordan Craters

FRENCHGLEN

The Castles

JORDAN VALLEY

95

ROME

TO THE EAST RIM OF STEENS MOUNTAIN

BACK ROAD TO FIELDS PAST STEENS MOUNTAIN

THROUGH THE CATLOW VALLEY AND HART MOUNTAIN ANTELOPE REFUGE

95

FIELDS

ADEL

140

Northwestern Oregon

Eastern Oregon

Southwestern Oregon

Eastern Oregon

OREGON

NEVADA

Eastern Oregon

The immensity of this region's mountains, canyons, rivers, plains and gorges, stretching out under a huge expanse of sky challenged my comprehension. Back roads here were longer, dustier, and often bumpier than those in western Oregon, but they were nevertheless just as well worth traveling. And it was like entering the "real" west with its cattle, coyotes, antelope, dust devils, cowboys, and tumbling-down early settlers' cabins.

Sunflower, Snake River road

Traveling the old Oregon Trail to Pendleton

Cara Neal said her barn had been painted with a
Bull Durham slogan in 1911, but within a year Dr. Pierce
came along with a better offer and the sign was
painted over.

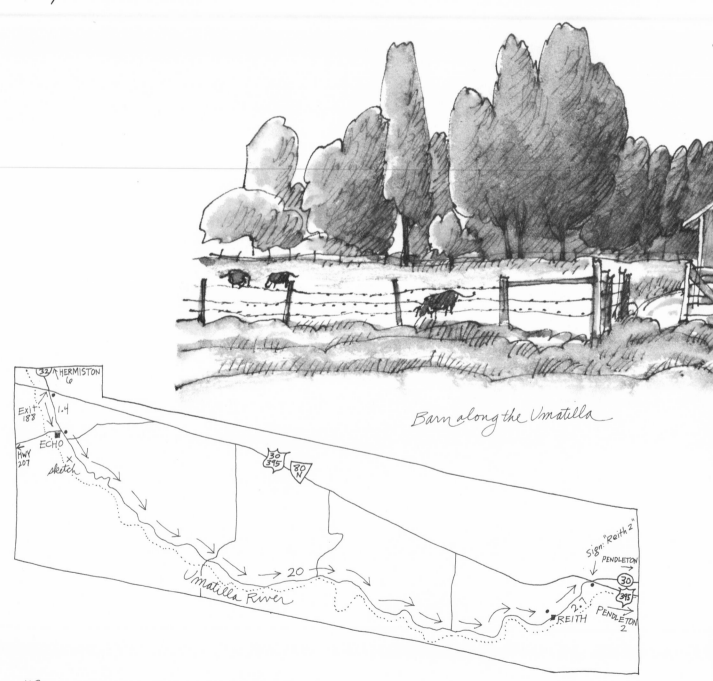

Barn along the Umatilla

The road past Echo was once the main
highway, but now only back road travelers can be
apprised of the doctor's Golden Medical Discovery.
The Umatilla runs past this road and
so do long, long freight trains.

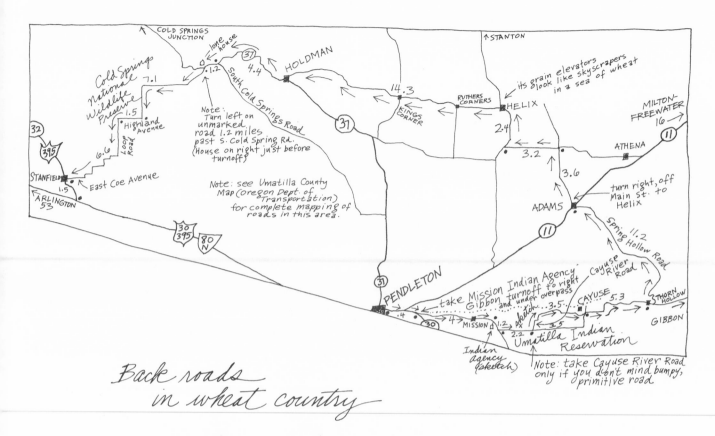

On the map:

↑ COLD SPRINGS JUNCTION
→ lone house
Ⓣ 37
4.4
HOLDMAN
↑ STANTON

its grain elevators look like skyscrapers in a sea of wheat

Cold Springs National Wildlife Preserve
7.1
1.5
0 1.2
South Cold Springs Road

Note: Turn left on unmarked road 1.2 miles past S. Cold Spring Rd. (House on right just before turnoff)

14.3
RUTHERS CORNERS
KINGS CORNER
HELIX
2.4

MILTON-FREEWATER 16 →
Ⓣ 11

Highland Avenue
Loop Road
6.6
Ⓣ 32
Ⓣ 395

3.2
ATHENA
3.6

STANFIELD
1.5
East Coe Avenue

turn right, off Main St. to Helix

Note: see Umatilla County Map (Oregon Dept. of Transportation) for complete mapping of roads in this area.

ARLINGTON 53

ADAMS
Ⓣ 11

Spring Hollow Road
11.2

Ⓣ 30 395
Ⓣ 80 N

Cayuse River Road

Ⓣ 31
PENDLETON
.4
Ⓣ 30
4
MISSION 1.2

take Mission Indian Agency Gibbon turnoff to right and under overpass
3.5
CAYUSE 5.3
THORN HOLLOW
GIBBON

2.2
3.5
Umatilla Indian Reservation

Indian agency (sketch)

Note: take Cayuse River Road only if you don't mind bumpy, primitive road.

Back roads in wheat country

On these roads long views of wheat
fields and the patterns that plowing them
makes delighted my eyes.
A totem pole adorns the entrance
to the Bureau of Interior Umatilla
Indian Reservation. The Indian worker
I asked about its origin said that it
had been constructed in the early 1930s
by CCC camp laborers at nearby Squaw
Creek. The talents of many went
into its creation. It has been
repainted several times, noses have
been replaced, and the base repaired,
so that the CCC totem still stands
tall at reservation headquarters.

Totem at the
Umatilla Indian
Agency

Wheat fields around Pendleton

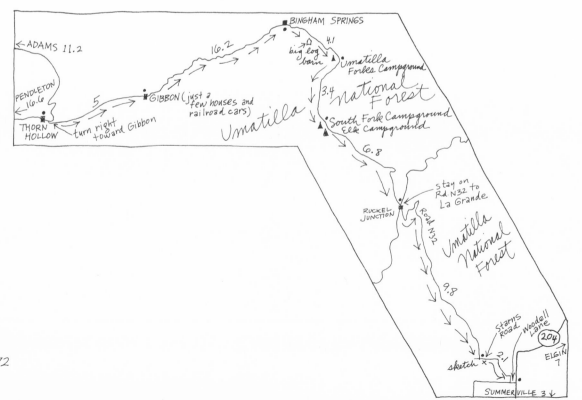

←ADAMS 11.2

PENDLETON 16.6→

THORN HOLLOW

turn right toward Gibbon

5

GIBBON (just a few houses and railroad cars)

16.2

BINGHAM SPRINGS

big log barn

4.1

Umatilla Forbes Campground

Umatilla

3.4 National Forest

South Fork Campground Elk Campground

6.8

RUCKEL JUNCTION

Stay on Rd. N32 to La Grande

Road N32

Umatilla National Forest

9.8

Starrs Road

Woodell Lane

204

ELGIN 7

sketch x

SUMMERVILLE 3↓

Through the Umatilla Forest to the Grande Ronde Valley

    By the time I reached Gibbon, forest trees were beginning to appear. I passed Bingham Springs, where there once had been a sulphur springs spa, and the Bar M Ranch with its great log barn.
    I continued on the mountain road through the forest to the spacious and fertile Grande Ronde Valley.

174

The Grande Ronde Valley

The road to
Hat Point Lookout

Stopping at the Ranger Station at
Joseph to check on road conditions, I was
handed a guide describing the trip to Hat Point.
There was a popular store at Imnaha, where
one could enjoy a cold drink before ascending
to or descending from Hat Point. The road to
the top was long and bumpy. The scenery,
however, made it all worthwhile.
I climbed the 100 steps to the tiny cabin of
Hat Point lookout tower where 7,072 feet above the
earth's surface at sea level, I had a view of the
Snake River in Hell's Canyon 1,250 feet below.

The view from Hat Point

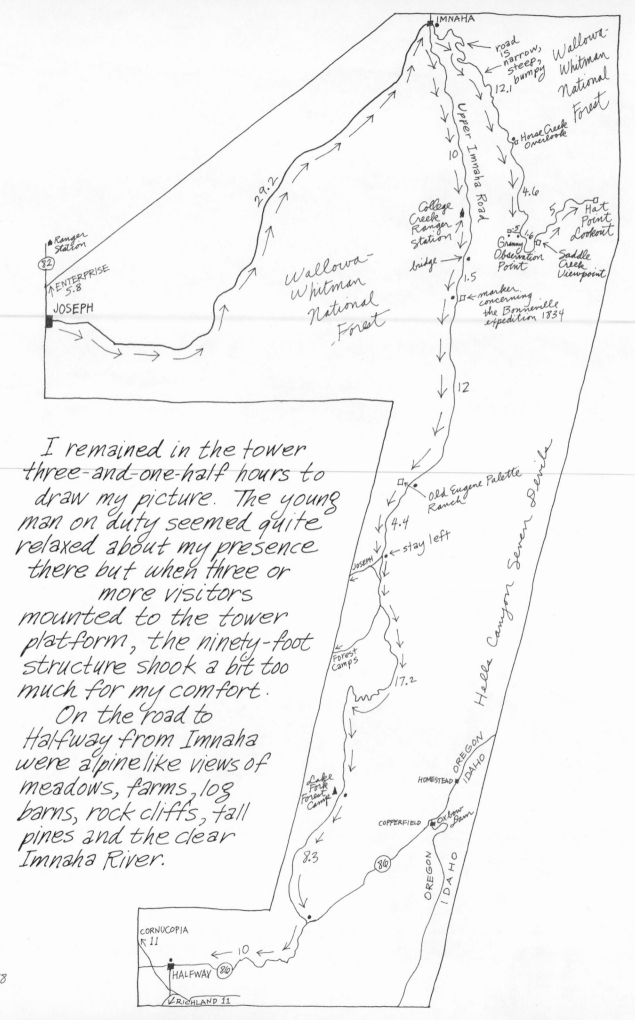

IMNAHA

road is narrow, steep, bumpy 12.1

Wallowa-Whitman National Forest

Horse Creek Overlook

Upper Imnaha Road

10

4.6

College Creek Ranger Station

5

Hat Point Lookout

Ranger Station

82

↑ENTERPRISE 5.8

JOSEPH

Wallowa-Whitman National Forest

bridge →

1.5

.5 1.6

Granny Observation Point

Saddle Creek Viewpoint

marker concerning the Bonneville expedition 1834

12

I remained in the tower three-and-one-half hours to draw my picture. The young man on duty seemed quite relaxed about my presence there but when three or more visitors mounted to the tower platform, the ninety-foot structure shook a bit too much for my comfort.

On the road to Halfway from Imnaha were alpine like views of meadows, farms, log barns, rock cliffs, tall pines and the clear Imnaha River.

Old Eugene Palette Ranch

4.4

← stay left

JOSEPH

Forest Camps

17.2

Hells Canyon Seven Devils

HOMESTEAD

OREGON IDAHO

Lake Fork Forest Camp

COPPERFIELD

Oxbow Dam

OREGON IDAHO

8.3

86

CORNUCOPIA ←11

← 10 ←

HALFWAY 86

↓RICHLAND 11

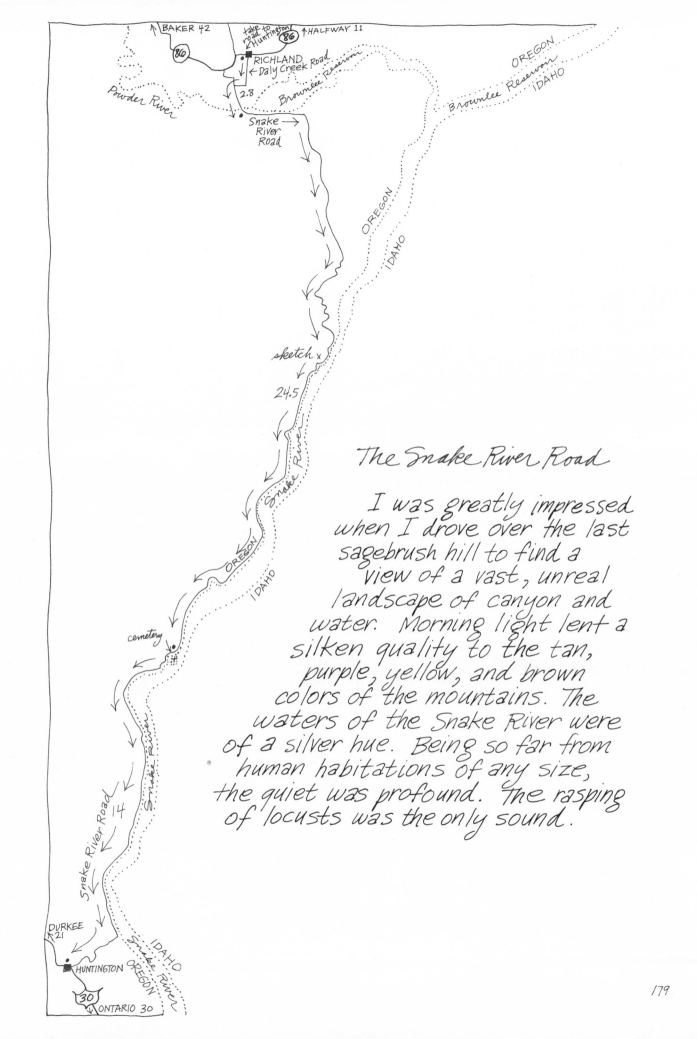

BAKER 42 ←

take to road Huntington

HALFWAY 11 ↑

86

RICHLAND

← Daly Creek Road

2.8

Brownlee Reservoir

OREGON

Brownlee Reservoir

IDAHO

Powder River

Snake River Road →

OREGON

IDAHO

sketch x

24.5

Snake River

OREGON

IDAHO

cemetery

Snake River Road 14

Snake River

DURKEE ← 21

IDAHO

Snake River

OREGON

HUNTINGTON

30

↓ ONTARIO 30

The Snake River Road

I was greatly impressed when I drove over the last sagebrush hill to find a view of a vast, unreal landscape of canyon and water. Morning light lent a silken quality to the tan, purple, yellow, and brown colors of the mountains. The waters of the Snake River were of a silver hue. Being so far from human habitations of any size, the quiet was profound. The rasping of locusts was the only sound.

The Snake River Road along the Oregon-Idaho-border

Driving through
Burnt River Canyon

I came upon many cattle
and sage grouse along the
road. The cattle would
stare, then turn and trot
ahead of me until I could
gently overtake them and
encourage them to one side.
A cowboy rounding up a small
herd told me "Ah'm jes'
taken' 'em up the road."
I sketched a flower along
here, the giant blazing star,
which has five white starlike
petals that open at night.

Giant
blazing star

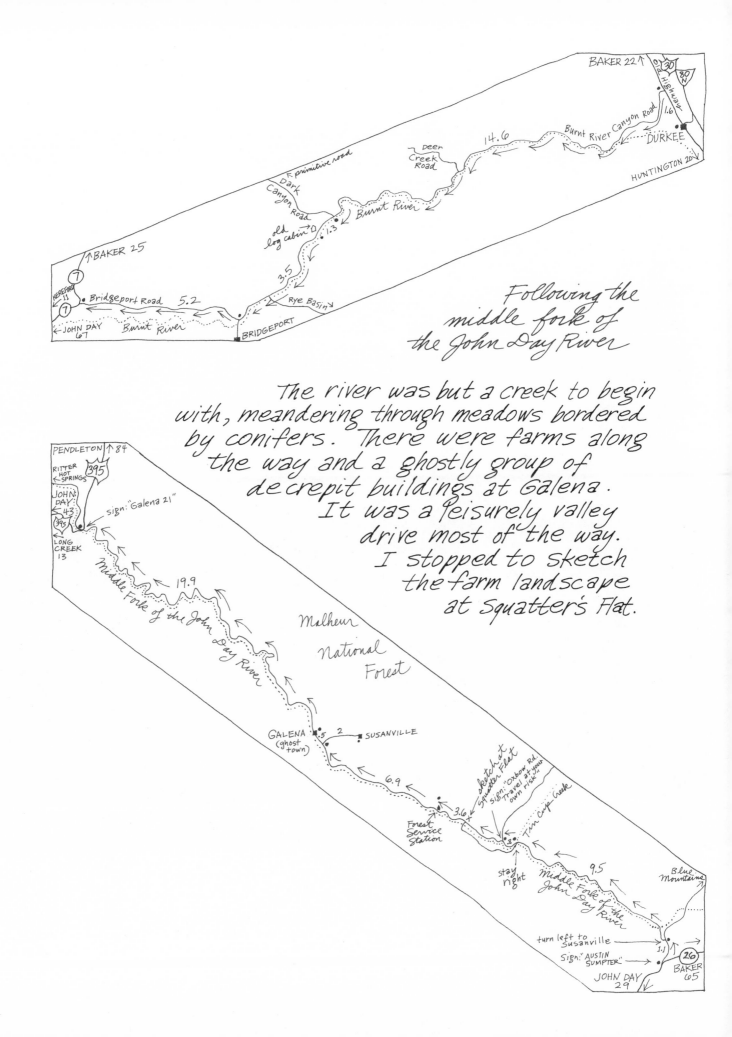

BAKER 22 ↑

12 Highway 30 N 80 N

Burnt River Canyon Road 1.6

DURKEE

HUNTINGTON 20 ↓

14.6

Deer Creek Road

primitive road

Dark Canyon Road

Burnt River

old log cabin 1.3

3.5

↑ BAKER 25

7
HEREFORD 11
7

• Bridgeport Road 5.2

Rye Basin

JOHN DAY 67 ← Burnt River

BRIDGEPORT

Following the
middle fork of
the John Day River

The river was but a creek to begin
with, meandering through meadows bordered
by conifers. There were farms along
the way and a ghostly group of
decrepit buildings at Galena.
It was a leisurely valley
drive most of the way.
I stopped to sketch
the farm landscape
at Squatter's Flat.

PENDLETON ↑ 84

395

RITTER HOT SPRINGS

JOHN DAY 43

395

LONG CREEK 13

Sign: "Galena 21"

Middle Fork of the John Day River

19.9

Malheur
National
Forest

GALENA (ghost town) .5   2   • SUSANVILLE

6.9

Forest Service Station

3.6

sketch at Squatter Flat
Sign: "Oxbow Rd. Travel at your own risk"

.8

Tin Cup Creek

stay right   Middle Fork of the John Day River

9.5

Blue Mountains

turn left to Susanville

Sign: "AUSTIN SUMPTER"

1.1

26
BAKER 65

JOHN DAY 29 ↓

Farm at Squatter's Flat along the middle fork of the John Day River

185

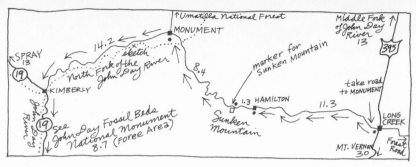

Off the main road past Sunken Mountain

In Oregon some back roads are much like highways. This fast back road passed a view of Sunken Mountain, which, did indeed seem to slip in the middle. The slow-paced village of Monument is surrounded by impressive rock formations. Just beyond the town I sketched the north fork of the John Day River as it flowed through the mountains.

North fork of the John Day River, near Monument

186

From the Painted Hills to Ashwood

I drew the ochres, yellows and reds of
Painted Hills in the early morning. It was a
challenge to represent so much color in
black and white!

↑MADRAS 33
↓MADRAS 35
ASHWOOD
↓Stud Horse Creek
6.9
↑ANTELOPE 17
Sign: "Mitchell 40 Horse Heaven Burnt Ranch"
10.8
HORSE HEAVEN
6.5
Cherry Creek Ranch
2
ford Cherry Creek
dramatic scenery
6.3
Byrds Point
John Day River
log bridge
5.9
Sign: ASHWOOD 36°
sketch
Painted Hills
1.3
sketch
State Park
5.6
6.1
FOSSIL 46 ↗
26
26
4.1
207
PRINEVILLE 44
MITCHELL

The scenery only got even better as I traveled the road to Ashwood. Views of Bridge Creek Valley, Byrd's Point, and the John Day River were a pleasure to behold. The road became more primitive after the last farm, until it reached Horse Heaven. It would not be good to travel this portion in wet weather.

Painted Hills

189

Prineville to Paulina,
Izee and Burns

There was the
Crooked River, farmland,
and the mountains of
Ochoco National Forest
to see on this trip.
At Glenn Place near
Paulina I sat in the
shade of tall Lombardy
poplars to sketch.
A great horned owl
peered out by the
window of the historic
old log house. It didn't
fly off but remained
to keep a blinking eye
on me.
Paulina had a frontier
town look with its little
church and assortment of
houses clustered near the
General Store.

Glenn Place

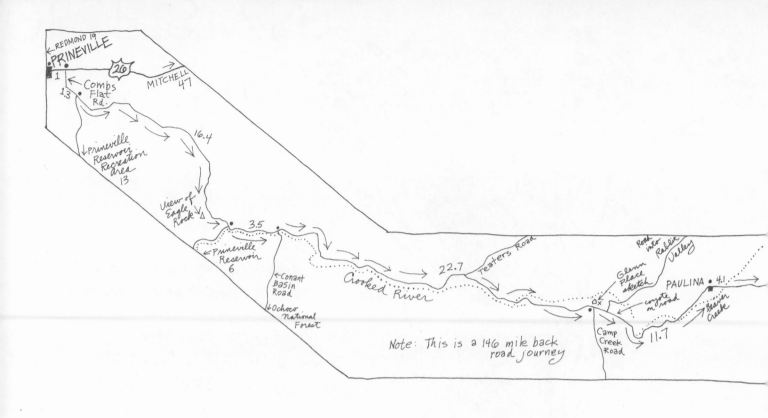

Note: This is a 146 mile back road journey

The Succor Creek Canyon Road and Leslie Gulch

The scenery was rugged with purplish brown crags that surrounded us campers in Succor Creek Canyon. It was late in the day. I cooked some dinner at the campground and watched the moon go down behind the high canyon walls. The only sound was cooing of doves from their perches among the high rocks.

Early next morning on the way to Leslie Gulch a herd of deer, including four large bucks, bounded gracefully across the road.

Leslie Gulch was a magnificent natural cathedral offering a treasury of highly colored and lofty rock creations for me to enjoy.

There were also the Jordan Craters close to the town of Jordan Valley and, near Rome, "the castles" to see.

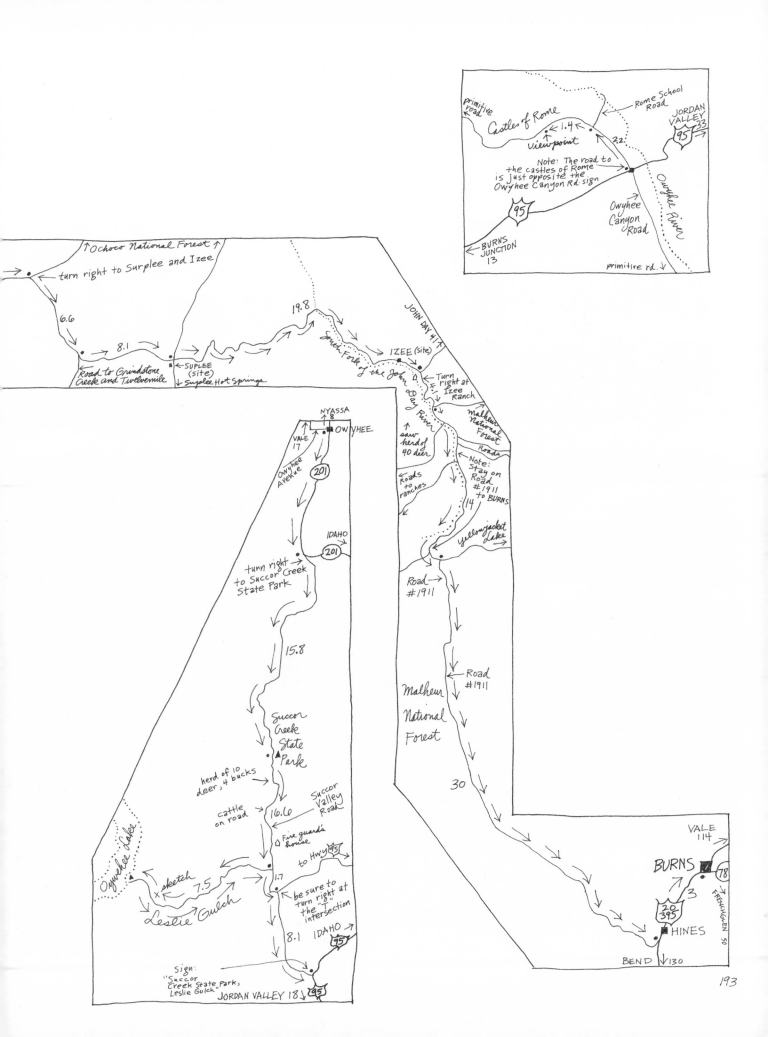

Inset map (top right):

primitive road

Castles of Rome

← 1.4

viewpoint

Rome School Road

JORDAN VALLEY 95 33

2.2

Note: The road to the castles of Rome is just opposite the Owyhee Canyon Rd. sign

95

← BURNS JUNCTION 13

Owyhee Canyon Road

Owyhee River

primitive rd. ↓

Main map:

↑Ochoco National Forest↑

turn right to Surplee and Izee

6.6

19.8

JOHN DAY 41

8.1

South Fork of the John Day River

IZEE (site)

Turn right at Izee Ranch

Road to Grindstone Creek and Twelvemile

SUPLEE (site)
↓ Suplee Hot Springs

saw herd of 40 deer

Malheur National Forest

Roads

Roads to ranches

Note: Stay on Road #1911 to BURNS

14

Yellowjacket Lake

Road #1911

NYASSA ↑ 8

VALE 17

OWYHEE

Owyhee Avenue

201

IDAHO 201

turn right to Succor Creek State Park

15.8

Road #1911

Malheur National Forest

30

Succor Creek State Park

herd of 10 deer, 4 bucks

cattle on road

16.6

Succor Valley Road

Owyhee Lake

Fire guard's house

to Hwy 95

sketch

7.5

1.7

be sure to turn right at the "T" intersection

Leslie Gulch

x

8.1 IDAHO 95

Sign: "Succor Creek State Park, Leslie Gulch"

JORDAN VALLEY 18 ↓ 95

VALE 114

BURNS 78

3

20 395

FRENCH-GLEN 50

HINES

BEND ↓ 130

193

Leslie Gulch

Back road to Fields
past Steen's Mountain

The great mass of Steen's
  Mountain rose to incredible
heights from the valley floor
  along this road. There were
occasional farms, and the
large Alvord Ranch. I found
it comforting to know that
I wasn't entirely alone on
  this sixty-five-mile stretch
  of dirt road!
    Farther on there was a big, big view of the
Alvord Desert and the mighty 9,000-foot Steen's
Mountain towering above.

Steen's Mountain

A lanky young man
in a high-domed, bluish gray
cowboy hat and cowboy boots
filled the gas tank of
my car at the general
store in the hamlet
of Fields.

BURNS
66 / 78

Sign:
Andrews 52
Fields 65
Denio 88

26.4
TO BURNS
JUNCTION

Juniper
Lake

27.4

Tudor
Lake

Note: Hwy 78 to
Fields is
64.5 miles
(gas at Fields)

Mann
Lake

Road to
Mann Lake
Ranch

views of
the great mountain

8.6

X
sketch

Alvord
Ranch

view of the great desert

14.2

Alvord
Desert

Wildhorse
Ranch
Road

ANDREWS
(site)

Alvord
Lake

12.4

FRENCHGLEN
49

Sign: Steen's Mt. Loop 38
Frenchglen 49
Burns

1.9

get gas at
old store
(1881)

FIELDS

DENIO 23

To the east rim of Steen's Mountain

At the base of the Steen's Mountain Loop was the tiny community of Frenchglen and its comfortable hotel. Still in operation, it was built in 1916 by the famous local cattle baron of that time, Pete French.

The drive up Steen's Mountain was deceptive in that it was such a gradual slope I didn't realize I was achieving great altitude. Passing from sagebrush country to juniper, to groves of aspen and to alpine wildflower strewn meadow told me I was certainly gaining altitude. Higher up there were spectacular views of glaciated valleys and from the east rim the large vista of the Alvord Desert over a mile below and all the land beyond.

BURNS 60 ↑

FRENCHGLEN 3.4

6.9 (205)

Hart Mountain

Antelope Refuge 35

3.2

Page Glen Campground

Start Steen's Mountain Road here (one way)

2.8 miles to Kiger Gorge view

15.4

Jackman Park Campground 4.2

East Rim View

5

16.9

herd of 15 wild horses

13.8

South Rim Road

9,600'

Roaring Springs Ranch

Blitzen Crossing

Steen's Mountain

35.4

HWY 78 64.5

1.4 FIELDS

DENIO 23

198

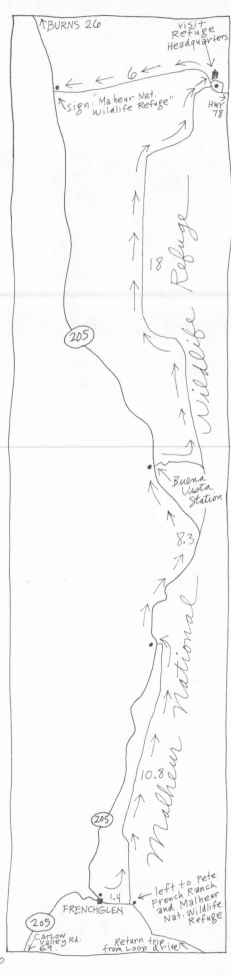

The road through
Malheur Wildlife Refuge

Though it was not March or April, when the largest concentrations of birds are present, I was able to see many varieties. These included Great Blue Herons, White Pelicans, Trumpeter Swans, Canada Geese, Long-billed Curlews, Great Egrets, Snowy Egrets, and many kinds of ducks and hawks.

President Theodore Roosevelt established this preserve in 1908. Ponds and crops are managed for the benefit of wildlife.

It was good to see a place dedicated to man's concern for nature. What would our earth be like without birds of all variety?

Trumpeter Swan

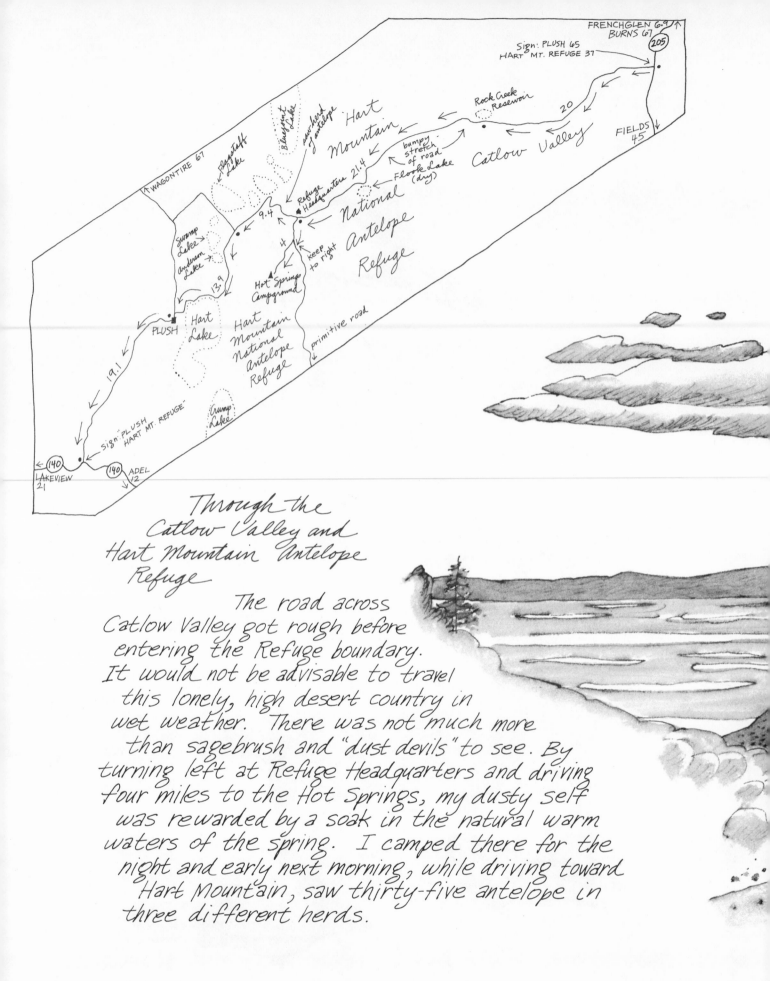

Through the Catlow Valley and Hart Mountain Antelope Refuge

The road across Catlow Valley got rough before entering the Refuge boundary. It would not be advisable to travel this lonely, high desert country in wet weather. There was not much more than sagebrush and "dust devils" to see. By turning left at Refuge Headquarters and driving four miles to the Hot Springs, my dusty self was rewarded by a soak in the natural warm waters of the spring. I camped there for the night and early next morning, while driving toward Hart Mountain, saw thirty-five antelope in three different herds.

Frightened by my vehicle they would run, then abruptly change direction, as if to confuse a hunter's aim. It was a thrill to see such beautiful animals in the wild.

View from Hart Mountain

Otis, my back
road advisor

Thoughts while traveling

It adds much to the remembrance of a place
to talk to local people. They would often
introduce themselves to me while I was sketching,
an opportunity to talk that I always welcomed.
I would also stop in the General Store to
shop and perhaps quench my thirst by drinking
something on the spot, returning the empty bottle to
the counter. Sometimes just being in a place for awhile
generates conversation. Checking road directions or
getting advice on what to see locally is another usually
successful way to begin a conversation with a stranger.

I believe that if one loves the earth and respects mankind one does not defile the land by throwing litter from an automobile.

I stayed in many motels in my travels through Oregon and those I appreciated most were neat, clean smelling and located away from highway noise. The owner's friendliness, flowers in the room (even just one or two) and a picture on the wall of good quality would make my home away from home all I could ask for.

Coming off a slow back road trip onto a busy highway, it is sometimes shocking to realize how fast and recklessly we have suddenly begun to travel.

I've become aware that the faster I drive the more I become an asphalt watcher. Driving is especially interesting and fun at slow speeds, for then I can enjoy the scenery. If there are many curves in the road I simply slow down even more. And on back roads I've noticed that many other drivers also seem to relax and enjoy the drive and the sights.

I'm remembering the route to Olallie Lake, a bumpy and twisted single lane road. The scenery was so close I could almost touch it. Ten miles per hour was maximum speed and though it was a narrow road, I knew that any traffic coming toward me was also limited by that speed so there was little likelihood of an accident.

I hope that road never changes. As soon as pavement and a double lane are put in, the road will be straightened, speed increased, and we will once again become asphalt watchers.

On dirt and gravel back roads I slowed down when meeting another vehicle to minimize the dust. I hoped that other drivers would do the same. Most often they did and we would both wave a greeting as we passed.

I wish more of Oregon's scenic back roads were in the one-way direction. Then they would not have to be wide, and more contact with nature would be felt. I'm thinking of the Grayback Ridge Motor Nature Trail near Crater Lake, a one-way road where I enjoyed a relaxing drive. I had more time to take in the sights than I would have otherwise. As Oregon's back roads are broadened and straightened for the needs of commerce, nature seems to retreat on all sides.

I found that many other drivers on back roads will wave as they go by. This is particularly true on less traveled roads. It is a wonderful way to indicate friendliness when an exchange of words isn't possible.

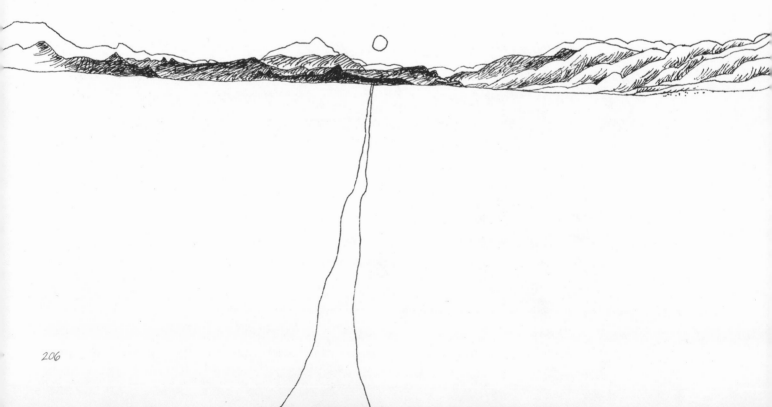